D Boyle

The Tenderness of God

D1260546

The Tenderness of God

Reclaiming Our Humanity

Gillian T. W. Ahlgren

Fortress Press
Minneapolis

THE TENDERNESS OF GOD
Reclaiming Our Humanity

Copyright © 2017 Fortress Press. All rights reserved. Except for brief quotations in critical articles or reviews, no part of this book may be reproduced in any manner without prior written permission from the publisher. Email copyright@1517.media or write to Permissions, Fortress Press, PO Box 1209, Minneapolis, MN 55440-1209.

Passages from *The Joy of the Gospel and Laudato Si': On Care for Our Common Home* are used here with permission © Libreria Editrice Vaticana.

Cover image: St. Francis Rejecting the World and Embracing Christ (red & black chalk on paper), Murillo, Bartolome Esteban (1618-82) / Hamburger Kunsthalle, Hamburg, Germany / Bridgeman.
Cover design: Laurie Ingram

Print ISBN: 978-1-5064-1052-4
eBook ISBN: 978-1-5064-1085-2

The paper used in this publication meets the minimum requirements of American National Standard for Information Sciences — Permanence of Paper for Printed Library Materials, ANSI Z329.48-1984.

Manufactured in the U.S.A.

This book was produced using Pressbooks.com, and PDF rendering was done by PrinceXML.

Most High, all glorious God,
enlighten the darkness of my heart.
Give me a right faith,
certain hope,
and perfect love,
with deep humility, wisdom and understanding,
that I may know and do
Your most holy will.

(Francis of Assisi)

Maybe we are all pilgrims and just don't know it.
We grow restless without meaning;
we yearn for integrity and truth
and something solid to believe in.
And as our wandering grows more deliberate and prayerful
the hunger for depth begins to take us to new places.

Pilgrimage is at least as much about
coming home to ourselves,
wherever we find ourselves,
as it is about leaving all that is comfortable to us
in order to discover that which
we've never seen or known before.

(Gillian Ahlgren, Spiritual Immersion Experience in Assisi)

*I dedicate this book
to Michael Joseph,
who helped create the space of tenderness
that I inhabit,
and to Daniel Francis,
just because.*

Contents

Contents

Introduction

Difficult times are always tender. They expose our fragility and make us wish that we were other than human. They put us in direct contact with our vulnerabilities and our fears, but they also reveal the strength, resilience, and possibility that reside beneath the surface of our lives. As I read the signs of our times, they qualify as "difficult," and we stand to lose a great deal. But is it possible that the very challenges that we face have the capacity to call us to a different way of experiencing our humanity? If we succumb to the posturing and violence that feed our anxieties, we stand to lose access to the very tenderness that sometimes frightens us with its beauty and potential. Is it time to try a different way?

The life of Francis of Assisi brilliantly shows us a revolutionary way of tenderness, open to us if we are willing to risk "falling in love in a quite absolute and final way."[1] Yet even for Francis, one of history's most beloved saints, this way of tenderness, authenticity, and joy was not obvious. As a young man, Francis wandered through a nagging dissatisfaction and emptiness until, as he himself tells us, "God led me

---

1. Cf. prayer associated with Pedro Arrupe, former Minister General of the Society of Jesus: "Nothing is more practical than finding God—that is, than falling in love in a quite absolute and final way. What you are in love with, what seizes your imagination, will affect everything. It will decide what will get you out of bed in the morning, what you do with your evenings, how you spend your weekends, what you read, whom you know, what breaks your heart, and what amazes you with joy and gratitude. Fall in love, stay in love, and it will decide everything."

among lepers."[2] In the place where he least expected it, Francis fell in love with the living God. And a whole new way of life began.

It is a way of life made universally visible by Jorge Bergoglio, the first pope to dare to assume the name "Francis," who now summons us to "the revolution of tenderness."[3] To many of us, such a revolution sounds not only attractive but also necessary in a world as needy as ours. But how and where does such a revolution begin? We have lost contact with nature. We have lost genuine connection with others; even our relationships with friends and loved ones are often stretched thin by daily stresses and are in need of deep renewal. We are beleaguered by the pace and challenges of daily living. Less patient, more abrasive, we are rendered all the more vulnerable to losing our very humanity.

As we lose touch with the basic qualities that keep us humane, imbue our human relationships with joy and possibility, and make life worth living, how can we learn the tender touch of the divine hand? Who will instruct us and guide the way?

We are fortunate to have the example of two individuals who, together and with radical complementarity, inspired a true "revolution" in their day. Francis (1182–1226) and Clare (1193–1253) of Assisi, two of Christianity's most well-known saints, were widely considered universal examples of human goodness during their day. Francis and Clare show us "just how inseparable the bond is between concern for nature, justice for the poor, commitment to society, and interior peace."[4] Their decision to live the gospel way in radical simplicity and purity of heart has not only inspired millions over the centuries but provides a viable way for us to recover the fullness of our humanity today.

Most importantly, Francis and Clare invite us to deepen our friendship with God—the One who walks with us; the One who shares

2. See Francis of Assisi, *Testament*, 2 in *The Saint*, ed. Regis J. Armstrong, J. A. Wayne Hellmann, and William J. Short, vol. 1 of *Francis of Assisi: Early Documents* (New York: New City Press, 1999), 124.
3. Pope Francis, *Joy of the Gospel* (Washington, DC: United States Conference of Catholic Bishops, 2013), par. 88.
4. Pope Francis, *Laudato Si': On Care for Our Common Home* (Washington, DC: United States Conference of Catholic Bishops, 2015), par. 10.

our burdens, our suffering, and our joy; and the One who gives us the hope, strength, and courage to work together toward a world that is truly home for all. This loving way of life that seeks encounter, collaboration, solidarity, and communion is articulated beautifully by Pope Francis, who reminds us that:

> Thanks solely to this encounter—or renewed encounter—with God's love, which blossoms into an enriching friendship, we are liberated from our narrowness and self-absorption. We become fully human when we become more than human, when we let God bring us beyond ourselves in order to attain the fullest truth of our being. . . . For if we have received the love which restores meaning to our lives, how can we fail to share that love with others?[5]

What will motivate us to set out on this way? Our own human needs and longings will move us there, especially as we grow more honest about them. We all need to love and be loved; we all long to love and be loved. There is nothing more practical or basic to humanity than that. When that need and that longing come together with sincerity, simplicity, and intensity, a new way of life comes alive. And that new way of life is more critical now than ever, for the world around us cries out its need for love and its need for tenderness.

We have the capacity to share life-giving love. This is the good news: that we can learn love, from God and from one another, as we share life together in graced encounter. Francis of Assisi's realization of God's nearness, known through the tenderness of loving human encounter, was the key to the revolutionary way of life still available to us today. Francis and Clare model for us "the revolution of tenderness," the gospel way that tells us to "risk face-to-face encounter with others, with their physical presence which challenges us, with their pain and their pleas, with their joy which infects us in our close and continuous interaction."[6] Learning to recognize and collaborate with the presence of God in the world around us gives us access to a joy no one can take from us.

5. Pope Francis, *Joy of the Gospel*, par. 8.
6. Ibid., par. 88.

Pope Francis reminds us that "we are called to bear witness to a constantly new way of living together in fidelity to the Gospel. Let us not allow ourselves to be robbed of community!"[7] To Pope Francis's plea I would add that we not allow ourselves to be robbed of the joy of life, the joy of being human and of sharing life together—the joy that is known and shared when we "fall in love and stay in love." Today we are even more confused than ever about what true joy is. And I suspect that such confusion stems from an even deeper uncertainty about love—what it is, where to find it, how to cultivate it, what to do when we no longer feel it. Love can neither be found nor shared alone. When we have lost the basic practices of community—meal sharing, fellowship, conversations about what matters most to us, and simply being present to one another—how can we expect to find what we most deeply long for? Our very humanity is being rewritten for us by the relentless demands of technology and a culture of consumerism. We need to recover the graces of a deeply relational culture in which we make time for meaningful companionship and create together the world we dream of.

In this book, I invite you to consider how we can, in our day and age, find together the living God—the One who walks with us as we create, with God and with one another, the life that we long for. Francis and Clare's path is one of radical simplicity that opens the heart and helps us to see what truly matters. Walking with them may give us new ways to engage our own challenges. Then, with a heart informed by the love of God, we can nurture the presence of God in one another and in our world. Let us not allow ourselves to be robbed of tenderness, of hearts that are true and strong, courageous and faithful. For when such hearts join together, infused by the energy of the Spirit, we are empowered in the love that provides hope, strength, and new possibility. Ultimately, this way of radical simplicity and sincerity frees us to collaborate in the work of renewing the face of the earth and making this world a true home for all.

7. Ibid., par. 92.

A Few Words about My Approach

As a professor of theology and a specialist in the Christian mystical tradition, I am always trying to find words that invite people to understand and experience God afresh. Francis and Clare continue to inspire new ways of seeing, new ways of praying, new ways of engaging the world, and there is a directness about their example that echoes the phrase attributed to Francis: "Preach the gospel at all times; use words when necessary." Historical context always sheds light on the challenges people face and the significance of their choices and decisions. The true genius of people's spiritual and theological insights is revealed as we walk with them through their life circumstances. The contours of their inner lives are illuminated by our knowledge of what they were up against. As we explore the world in which Francis and Clare lived, we are likely to find many parallels with the economic, political, and even religious turbulence that we face today. Their wisdom will shine forth with new radiance as we encounter them anew as human beings just like us.

I am an academic, trained at the University of Chicago in the history of Christianity and have been teaching the Christian mystical tradition to people of all ages and walks of life for over twenty-five years. Teaching theology has taught me that theology must be constantly tested and proven through concrete spiritual, ethical, and human applications. When we are in darkness and confusion, theology should offer light. Theology derives its power and authority from its capacity to illuminate and provide meaning, to move us toward greater freedom and responsiveness to the Spirit, and to speak prophetically to our contemporary circumstances. Theology should empower us to integrate the wisdom of our past in order to address the urgent challenges of today.

Francis and Clare breathed theology. Because they aspired to live constantly in the presence of God, they teach us how relevant theology can be. Francis and Clare were wise, mature, and integrated people, as fully in possession of their minds, hearts, and wills as human beings can be. They did not make grandiose distinctions between the challenges of the external world and their own inner struggles, between "history" and "spirituality." They did not see "theology" as something other than their daily attempt to live out the gospel and their whole-hearted love of God and creation in ordinary ways. Their insights and exhortations are as challenging and life-giving as we, their heirs, will allow them to be. Rather than domesticating their message with our own ideological, disciplinary, or institutional agendas, I suggest that we allow them to speak on their own terms, granting their voices the authority they deserve. This book attempts to facilitate that process, giving voice to a powerful legacy that had revolutionary implications for their times, just as it does for us today.

As we listen to their message, I ask you to remember that whenever I use the word "Franciscan," I am referring to both Francis and Clare. Indeed, the Franciscan tradition is misunderstood and misrepresented if it does not thoroughly and completely integrate the insights and visions of both Clare and Francis. We should consider them cofounders of this revolution of tenderness. However, this approach is not reflected in much of the earlier (and even some of the more recent) scholarship. Joan Mueller rightly points out that "when reading histories of the early Franciscan movement, one cannot help but wonder, 'Where are the women?'"[1] Franciscan histories of the past, as

---

1. See Joan Mueller, *The Privilege of Poverty: Clare of Assisi, Agnes of Prague, and the Struggle for a Franciscan Rule for Women* (University Park: Pennsylvania State University Press, 2006), viii, where she also observes: "To put it simply, the common perception of early Franciscan women is that they were enclosed in the silence of their spiritually rich but historically inconsequential lives." Margaret Carney makes a similar observation when she says that the absence of material on Clare and her sisters in religious life "indicates an inadequate appreciation . . . of the historical role

well as biographies of the present, suffer radical inadequacies when they focus on the male branch of the movement. Historical accuracy requires us to recognize the presence of women in the movement from the outset.[2] The way of life that we call "Franciscan" could not have evolved in the way that it did had Clare not joined Francis, adding her own indelible contours to the revolution of tenderness. The full charism of the Franciscan way of life, with all of its theological and spiritual implications, cannot be appropriated without an integrated synthesis of their shared vision of the gospel life.[3] It is certainly my hope that this study elicits a more integrated, accurate, and inclusive approach from here on out.

In insisting on a deeper synthesis and integration, I am not suggesting that Francis's and Clare's journeys or perspectives were identical. For as much as they shared values, visions, and commitments, and for as much support as they gave one another, each approached relationship with God differently, and each faced different responses, both from their own immediate religious communities and from the institutional church more generally. But Franciscan studies have reached a point in which we must acknowledge what Margaret Carney has rightly called "the *shared* vocation of Francis and Clare,"[4] a vocation to holiness, to prophetic action, to leadership, and to the project of being human that we, too, male and female, must share and develop mutually.

The message of Francis and Clare, like that of the One whom they followed, is both demanding and liberating. To let Francis and Clare speak to us directly is to listen to a message that, like the gospel, will

played by these women." See Margaret Carney, *The First Franciscan Woman: Clare of Assisi and Her Form of Life* (Quincy, IL: Franciscan Press, 1993), 14.

2. For a graphic representation of this reality, see the map of Poor Ladies' convents in 1228 in Armstrong et al., *The Saint*, 200.

3. The complementarity of male and female religious reformers beginning in the thirteenth century signals what Bernard McGinn has called the "new mysticism," about which he writes: "Nothing is more striking about the new mysticism beginning about 1200 than the important role that women assume" and "Just as remarkable as the sudden emergence of women at this time is the evidence that this emergence was characterized by new forms of cooperation between women and men, in terms of both a shared dedication to the pursuit of the *vita apostolica* and a joint concern for attaining the 'loving knowledge of God.'" Bernard McGinn, *The Flowering of Mysticism: Men and Women in the New Mysticism—1200-1350* (New York: Crossroad, 1988), 15, 17.

4. Carney, *First Franciscan Woman*, 62.

change who we are. Their words point to a more authentic way of living out our relationship with God and with one another. If we find Francis and Clare's spirituality authentic, then we must listen to what they have to teach us about God. For their God is a God who might surprise us; the Christian community they invite us to join is one that might look somewhat different from the one we are currently a part of. Francis and Clare asked their contemporaries to do hard things: to reach out in love to the leper and the marginalized; to recognize, in poverty and simplicity, the face of Christ in the other; to move past superficialities in order to find and revere, protect, and defend the God who is pulsing in the heart of a suffering world.

Having walked in the footsteps of Francis and Clare with students in Assisi for many years, and now looking with renewed hope and joy at the winds of changes that Pope Francis brings to our world, I decided that it was the appropriate time to weave some of my reflections from prayerful moments in Assisi and La Verna into this narrative so that you can see the profound impact that they have had on my own understanding of God. These passages appear in italics in each chapter, as an integral part of this text. I hope that this book offers a theological and spiritual synthesis of contemporary relevance. I would like to thank those who have walked with me, over the years, on the Spiritual Immersion Experiences I lead; our conversations have been critical to the slow process of finding words for what matters most to us. I would also like to thank the Louisville Institute for their Sabbatical Grants for Researchers, which allowed me to grow into a deeper understanding of the impact of trauma on Francis and Clare and the ways that their life narratives and practices can help trauma survivors. Finally, I would like to thank the Dean of the College of Arts and Sciences at Xavier University and our Faculty Development Committee for awarding me a research sabbatical for this work. Whether this serves as your initial introduction to the lives of Francis and Clare or whether you have already been drawn closer to God because of them, I hope that this book serves as food for your ongoing journey.

1

Becoming a Pilgrim People: Journeying Together

Yet unless they go in search for God,
they will not find God,
no matter how much they cry for God.
(John of the Cross, *Spiritual Canticle*)

We sense the challenge of finding and sharing a "mystique" of living
together, of mingling and encounter, of embracing and supporting one
another, of stepping into this flood tide which, while chaotic, can become
a genuine experience of fraternity, a caravan of solidarity, a sacred
pilgrimage. (Pope Francis, *Joy of the Gospel*)

What happens when we take seriously our sense that there has to be
something more to our lives than what we are currently experiencing?
Whenever we instinctually know that our lives, individually and
collectively, are not entirely working, our dissatisfaction, whether with
our personal circumstances or with the world in which we live, can
become the seed of change and creative possibility. We need not use
religious language to describe this deeply human instinct. We need
only recognize, with sincerity and integrity, the desire for greater
meaning, coherence, and purpose in our lives. And then, for the sake of

our own well-being, we must engage a genuine process of searching, a journey that leads us to probe what it means to be human and how to be related to others. For as we begin to speak more honestly about our longings for fullness of life, we often come to find out that we are not alone in them.

The Irish spiritual writer John O'Donohue called this process of longing our way to greater connection with others "belonging," and, as he tells us:

> Belonging is deep; only in a superficial sense does it refer to our external attachment to people, places and things. It is the living and passionate presence of the soul. Belonging is the heart and warmth of intimacy. When we deny it, we grow cold and empty. Our life's journey is the task of refining our belonging so that it may become more true, loving, good and free. We do not have to force belonging. The longing within us always draws us towards belonging, and again towards new forms of belonging, when we have outgrown the old ones. Post-modern culture tends to define identity in terms of ownership: possessions, status and qualities. . . . [But] true belonging is gracious receptivity. This is the appropriate art of belonging in friendship—where friends do not belong *to* each other, but rather *with* each other. . . . True belonging comes from within. It strives for a harmony between the *outer* forms of belonging and the inner music of the soul. We seem to have forgotten the true depth and spiritual nature of intimate Belonging.[1]

O'Donohue underscores for us the hopeful good news about being human: the hungers of our hearts intuitively know what truly feeds us and what does not. But it can take quite a bit of work and discipline to orient our daily lives around what is truly life-giving. Honestly distinguishing between what we most deeply want and what we so readily settle for is a great help in discarding what keeps us from being free to create the life that we long for. Sometimes the very circumstances of our lives force us to ask ourselves with compelling urgency what truly matters to us and what does not. The very chaos of our current reality awakens us to our need for meaning and coherence, which turns out to be nearly as critical as our daily bread.

For both Francis and Clare, their dissatisfaction with life reached

---

1. John O'Donohue, *Eternal Echoes: Exploring Our Hunger to Belong* (New York: Bantam, 2000), 3–4.

in deep. Their journey toward a life of purpose, meaning, and joy epitomizes Saint Augustine's succinct observation about the human condition: "Our hearts are restless until they find their rest in You" (*Confessions*, 1.1). They model for us how to live out the spiritual journey with integrity as "pilgrim people"—people who seek to move forward, step by step, toward a more humane world, a more authentic human community. As a person who has led pilgrimages for many years, I have been privileged to accompany people in this process of leaving behind the norms of ordinary life in search of the "something more" they long for. And what we discover as we journey together is always far more than what we could imagine alone.

The Pilgrimage Experience

Every religious tradition has sacred spaces that commemorate special moments of encounter with the divine. We call the people who go to them pilgrims. All human beings are pilgrim people. We are constantly searching for meaning. We want coherence and order, even as we often need to disrupt the ordinary and mundane in order to reconnect with what matters to us. In so far as each one of us hungers for something more, we are all pilgrims.

I have engaged regularly in some form or another of pilgrimage since my first trip to Europe when I was nineteen years old. In fact, I am a church historian and theologian in large part because of that journey. On that first trip, without knowing who Ignatius Loyola was nor why he, too, had visited the Benedictine monastery of Montserrat, I looked up at the serrated mountains above the complex and felt somehow a part of something much greater than I was. The same thing happened as I circled very slowly around the choir of the cathedral of Chartres, gazing at scene after scene of the life of Christ, illuminated by the colored light of sunshine streaming through stained glass windows. Why would a whole city devote its intellectual, artistic, technological, economic, and human resources toward the construction of a cathedral? I found myself filled with questions about what it means to be human, why we do what we do, and whether or not (and how), as humans, we come to know God. The questions I brought home with me after that first pilgrimage experience were greeted with encouragement by both professors who mentored me and friends who explored them with me. They led me to doctoral work in the history of Christianity and in the Christian mystical tradition. As I have encountered a whole community of people, past and present, who asked the deepest questions that human beings can ask, I have sought to share those same questions with others in the community. And so the journey continues, year after year.

Since 1999, I have engaged the transformative tradition of pilgrimage more intentionally by taking groups of people on immersion experiences to Assisi and La Verna in the footsteps of Francis and Clare. Each time I go, I am privileged to watch people fall in love—with life and, often, with God. This is a phenomenon that, over each year, grows more and more predictable in the groups I shepherd. Experiencing together Francis and Clare's simplicity and sincerity helps all of us to fall in love with the goodness of life. Over the years, I have seen how our experiences of walking together in intentional community can help people negotiate significant challenges with deeper grace and energy, can renew love relationships, and can provide people with the inspiration and strength to change careers or make other critical life decisions.

It does not necessarily take engaging a physical pilgrimage to find meaning or to fall in love with God. But it does take leaving behind, in some significant way, the self that we have constructed up to this particular moment of our lives, so that we are free and open to being touched by God in new ways. To claim our identity as pilgrims is to wean ourselves from personal and social markers of identity, choosing instead to define ourselves as being on a journey to reclaim our souls.[2]

2. Parker Palmer puts this process beautifully when he writes: "We arrive in this world with birthright gifts—then we spend the first half of our lives abandoning them or letting others disabuse us of them. As young people, we are surrounded by expectations that may have little to do with who we really are, expectations held by people who are not trying to discern our selfhood but to fit us into slots. In families, schools, work places, and religious communities, we are trained away from true self toward images of acceptability; under social pressures like racism and sexism our original shape is deformed beyond recognition; and we ourselves, driven by fear, too often betray true self to gain the approval of others. We are disabused of original giftedness in the first

It is the "going out" of the smallness of ourselves that is critical. Indeed, if we are not willing to leave behind elements of the self and the smallness of our own perspectives in order to grow and be changed, we will never truly engage pilgrimage, no matter how far we travel.

If we want to find the love that gives meaning to our lives, we must own a process of inquiry, exploration, and change. The first step in finding what we want is to actively seek it. This requires us to go outside the self. Ironically, in the life of the Spirit, it takes leaving the self to actually find the self. A common refrain within mystical texts is that our search for God is, at the same time, a search for our authentic selves. The fundamental hypothesis in this search—one that is confirmed after we have first taken the risk of testing it in our own experience—is that we are created for relationship, with God and one another. This is not simply a "faith statement"; it is a premise about our humanity that each of us, for our own well-being, needs to test and explore in the laboratory of life. The journey toward our authentic humanity is a communal one and God reveals Godself to us in new and surprising ways as we seek God's presence in our own lived experience. "The Lord your God is in your midst," writes the prophet Zephaniah (Zeph 3:17); pilgrimage is the journey toward discovering that reality for ourselves.

The Theme of Journeying in the Gospels

The life of Jesus as it is portrayed in the Gospels manifests love in action. In Mark, for example, Jesus is portrayed as moving throughout Galilee, teaching and healing, surrounded by companions, and constantly in contact with people. Early on, this same lifestyle of journeying "two by two . . . taking nothing for the journey" (Mark 6:7–8) became the norm for Jesus's companions, who went forth to share healing and hope in imitation of what they themselves had been learning. Women and men gave testimony to what they had

half of our lives. Then—if we are awake, aware, and able to admit our loss—we spend the second half trying to recover and reclaim the gift we once possessed." Parker Palmer, *Let Your Life Speak: Listening for the Voice of Vocation* (San Francisco: Jossey-Bass, 2000), 12.

experienced through their contact with Jesus; Pope Francis is clear to remind us that the work of "missionary discipleship" is a vocation shared by all the baptized.[3] The Samaritan woman who conversed with Jesus at Jacob's well drew many Samaritans toward Jesus, and they first came to believe in him "because of the woman's testimony."[4] (John 4:39) And the first several chapters of Acts reiterate this model of a community in constant action, men and women, gathered and going forth, sharing their possessions and bearing witness, in word and in deed, to the love of God.[5] Conversion and transformation happen through the lived experience of God in our midst, just as the disciples realized on the road to Emmaus. As they reflected together and remembered, they knew: were not our hearts burning within us?

After his decision to embrace the gospel life, it was with great joy that Francis of Assisi heard particular passages from scripture, receiving them as instructions for his new form of life:

> When he heard that Christ's disciplines should not possess gold or silver or money, or carry on their journey a wallet or a sack, nor bread nor a staff, nor to have shoes nor two tunics, but that they should preach the reign of God and reconciliation, the holy man Francis, immediately exulted in the spirit of God. "This is what I want!" he said. "This is what I seek, this is what I desire with all my heart."[6]

"Overflowing with joy," Francis's biographer Thomas of Celano tells us, he "hastened to implement the words . . . and was careful to carry them out to the letter."[7] Francis wanted to model the simple, itinerant lifestyle that Jesus taught, knowing that it was critical in order to "give

---

3. Pope Francis, *Joy of the Gospel* par. 120: "In virtue of their baptism, all the members of the People of God have become missionary disciples (cf. Matt 28:19). All the baptized, whatever their position in the Church or their level of instruction in the faith, are agents of evangelization. . . . The new evangelization calls for personal involvement on the part of each of the baptized. Every Christian is challenged, here and now, to be actively engaged in evangelization; indeed, anyone who has truly experienced God's saving love does not need much time or lengthy training to go out and proclaim that love. Every Christian is a missionary to the extent that he or she has encountered the love of God in Christ Jesus: we no longer say that we are 'disciples' and 'missionaries,' but rather that we are always 'missionary disciples.'"

4. Pope Francis uses the same example in *Joy of the Gospel*, par. 120.

5. Cf. Acts 2:13–14, 2:42–47, and esp. 4:32–35.

6. Thomas of Celano, *The Life of St. Francis*, 1:9:22, in Armstrong et al., *The Saint*, 201–2.

7. Ibid.

good example to everyone" and show that "they were of one mind in the love of God and neighbor," truly apostolic people of the gospel.[8]

The framework of "walking with one another in the presence of God" is what best characterizes this way of proceeding, as companions to one another along the way. Companions break bread together; this is the literal meaning of the word "companion." In English, we derive the word "accompaniment" from the same root as "companions," and it points to our willingness to walk with and accompany others through all the phases and challenges of their lives. When we break bread together, we share with one another what we have, but, more importantly, we share who we are. And all of us emerge the richer, the wiser, and the more empowered for it. Likewise, pilgrims truly care for one another; their journey to discover the God in their midst is concurrently one of self-sharing. On the journey, we share our stories. In a community of other seekers, we confide our questions, our doubts, and our dreams. We receive encouragement in our growth, insights from others, and, most importantly, we come to understand that we are never alone on the way. "Accompaniment" is, more than anything, what pilgrims learn in a true pilgrimage: how to walk with one another in such a way that our walking together helps us to grow, together, toward the God who is known in our midst.

Humbly and with great vision and hope, Pope Francis states quite clearly that all of us will need to learn anew "the art of accompaniment." For accompaniment is both the way of the gospel and the best way of being human. He writes:

> The Church will have to initiate everyone—priests, religious and laity—into this "art of accompaniment" which teaches us to remove our sandals before the sacred ground of the other (cf. Exod 3:5). The pace of this accompaniment must be steady and reassuring, reflecting our closeness and our compassionate gaze which also heals, liberates and encourages growth in the Christian life.[9]

---

8. See *A Mirror of Perfection of the Status of a Lesser Brother*, 3:71, in *The Prophet*, vol. 3 of *Francis of Assisi: Early Documents*, ed. Regis J. Armstrong, J. A. Wayne Hellmann, and William J. Short (New York: New City Press, 2001), 316.
9. Pope Francis, *Joy of the Gospel*, par. 169.

Genuine accompaniment always adds meaning to our lives. When our questions, our doubts, and our struggles are acknowledged and honored, we realize that we are courageously moving toward greater and greater authenticity. When our gifts, our insights, and our growth are affirmed, we see ourselves making progress toward the persons we strive to be. Claiming our identity as "pilgrims" who seek to live more meaningfully and more purposefully, contributing to the common good of the human race is a helpful way of bringing greater coherence to our lives as human beings.

The suggestion here is that genuine accompaniment, like genuine pilgrimage, brings a helpful and productive fruitfulness to our lives. We find happiness and fulfillment through journeying together because we gain clarity about the meaning and purpose of our lives and because we are offering others what is meaningfully unique about us—what we were brought into this world to share with others. Sharing the journey gives us deeper insight into who we are meant to be. In *Let Your Life Speak: Listening for the Voice of Vocation*, Parker Palmer offers a helpful description of our gradual growth toward how our human potential. For Palmer, this process requires attending to how we appropriate lessons from each life experience. Palmer writes:

> Vocation does not come from willfulness. It comes from listening. I must listen to my life and try to understand what it is truly about—quite apart from what I would like it to be about—or my life will never represent anything real in the world, no matter how earnest my intentions. That insight is hidden in the word *vocation* itself, which is rooted in the Latin for "voice." Vocation does not mean a goal that I pursue. It means a calling that I hear. Before I can tell my life what I want to do with it, I must listen to my life telling me who I am. I must listen for the truths and values at the heart of my own identity. . . . Behind this understanding of vocation is a truth that the ego does not want to hear because it threatens the ego's turf: everyone has a life that is different from the "I" of daily consciousness, a life that is trying to live through the "I" who is its vessel. This is what the poet knows and what every wisdom tradition teaches: there is a great gulf between the way my ego wants to identify me, with its protective masks and self-serving fictions, and my true self.[10]

10. Palmer, *Let Your Life Speak*, 4–5.

To go on pilgrimage is to engage more deliberately in a process of searching and growing. A pilgrimage is both an individual experience and a communal one. This is why the pilgrim is a helpful metaphor both to describe the individual searcher as well as the universal church, even the entire human species. We are constantly learning who we are in light of the relationships that form our being. For the believer, relationship with the divine is the overarching relationship that provides meaning. And yet, even the believer must constantly return to ask the question of who, exactly, we are in a relationship with and how that relationship is developing at any given moment. Or, to put it another way, the ancient human question "Who am I?" leads inevitably to the equally important question "Whose am I?"[11] To whom do I belong, and how does that belonging form and shape me?

Allowing God to reveal Godself to us in ever new ways and on the terms that God chooses (not the ones we try to impose on our relationship with God) is surprising and revelatory. The "pedagogy of God," or the many ways that God illuminates our understanding, never ceases to peck away at, even shatter, whatever deception we are currently laboring under—if we let it. With clarity and compassion, the tender touch of the divine hand indicates all spaces where we can (must?) continue to grow and makes clear the many ways that our actions contradict God's loving intent for us and for our world. Our willingness to respond to God's constant encouragement to grow toward greater integrity then invites us to embody, all the more thoroughly, God's loving vision of justice, dignity, and fullness of life for all. Pope Francis uses the word "docile," meaning a "docility to the Spirit," in his *Joy of the Gospel*, and for some the word may have an unfortunate connotation. Although we may think of "docility" as passive, more than anything, docility is a deep responsiveness to the love of God that invites us to grow. "Docile" traces its root back to the word "to teach," and it actually means that we are "teachable," or willing to learn—in this case, from God and from life. We have all heard of "the teachable moment," in a classroom or even in a family

11. Ibid., 17.

conversation, when something happens or something is said that creates an opportunity to examine or explore our experience and learn something profound from it. To live our lives in such a constantly teachable way, always willing to learn something new and grow in response to what we learn, reflects our growing sensitivity to the movements of the Spirit, in ourselves and in our world, as well as a deepening commitment and attunement to the invitation of God in every moment. What a relief to know that "God's presence accompanies the sincere efforts of individuals and groups to find encouragement and meaning in their lives."[12]

Saint Augustine famously called us "pilgrim people." There is something sacred about our walking together, for in sincere togetherness we create new paths. Indeed, it is in taking the risk to set out on a journey with others, in search of the Something More that we long for, that life really begins.

Engaging the Journey: A Stop at Greccio

In retracing the journeys of Francis and Clare—following in their footsteps as it were—we come to know and understand the contours of their spiritual lives. This means we are participating in an ancient tradition of pilgrimage, even as we reshape it in the terms that make the most sense to us as modern and postmodern people. While a pilgrimage is (and was, historically) a physical act involving travel to a distant destination, it is also a deeply spiritual act. We leave behind all that "marks" and identifies us in the world in order to enter, more anonymously, into our truest identity as human persons. We enter into our hearts, especially those tender inner spaces that have become hardened and encrusted—perhaps even lost to us—by the fray of the day to day. And we enter into our souls, which we may have never even claimed as our deepest birthright in God. For in what sense does the world we inhabit encourage us to own the depths of our souls and live from their wisdom?

On pilgrimage in Italy, as soon as we land in Rome, we board our charter bus immediately toward Assisi, always stopping, about halfway, at the lovely

---

12. See Pope Francis, *Joy of the Gospel*, par. 71.

Franciscan monastery in Greccio. The bus ride is a chance for us to consider that our pilgrimage is a unique time set aside to let our souls be touched by experiences of insight, discovery, and realization, both through novelty and through familiarity. To be a pilgrim, we realize, as the bus begins to ascend the hillside toward the monastery of Greccio, is to engage a journey of the mind, heart, and senses that makes us aware of the sacredness of life.

Greccio epitomizes how Francis constantly sought to help his contemporaries see God in very familiar ways, for it was in Greccio, late in his life, that he organized a reenactment of Jesus's birth. By seeing God in the poverty of a naked infant and in the community of love that surrounded the manger, Francis invited people into a deeper awareness of the presence of God that emerges all the more clearly in our radical simplicity. In his reenactment of the birth of Jesus, Francis hoped to recall for them the fragility of that moment of birth and the reality that we share, in our human vulnerability, something with a God who chose to share all that it is to be human. As Donald Dunson writes:

> From the very first moment that the hands of another human being lift us from the womb, we must rely on others to feed us, protect us, teach us, and love us into life. This is our fate. This is what it means to be human. . . . Our mutual need is both human and holy.[13]

Of the many images at the sanctuary in Greccio, perhaps the most striking one is a woodcut of the earliest Franciscans attending to lepers in the leper colony. Their reverent attention to the bodily needs of their brothers and sisters manifests a tenderness and loving kindness that is palpable, humbling, and powerful. Francis was unafraid to accept his own vulnerability as a source of commonality, even of communion. He opened up this way to his contemporaries and to us today, having learned how to share vulnerability among the lepers he called sisters and brothers.

---

13. Donald Dunson, *No Room at the Table: Earth's Most Vulnerable Children* (Maryknoll, NY: Orbis Press, 2003), 4.

Image 1a. Transforming a Leper Colony into a Space of Loving Kindness (Image from the Sanctuary of Greccio).

Stopping at Greccio is an important entry into the reality of the incarnation, the profound demonstration that God is with us, through thick and thin, no matter what. This intimate solidarity helps us to see God anew, to believe that we can become people we have never yet been, and to believe that we are loved and are lovable.[14] The residual peace at Greccio helps us sense the invitation to this new view of a God who emerges tenderly in our midst. Quietly we receive an invitation to new life that comes from God's gentle presence there. Our journey has begun.

14. Cf. Roch Niemier, *In the Footsteps of Francis and Clare* (Cincinnati: St. Anthony Messenger Press, 2006), 153.

2

Searching for Meaning: Disruption and the Need for Connection

Some time when the river is ice ask me
mistakes I have made. Ask me whether
what I have done is my life.[1]

God's own dwelling in our midst fosters "solidarity, fraternity, and the desire for goodness, truth and justice."[2] And yet we live in a world oriented toward competition, superficiality, indifference, and even violence—forces that can splinter us within and disconnect us from one another. Is it any wonder that we feel in our hearts, our psyches, and our very bones the many contradictions of our reality as human persons? But what if dissatisfaction and disillusionment, as disorienting as they can be, are actually spiritual indicators of our own need for radical change? Can confusion or even distress, when addressed honestly and within safe relational contexts, constitute an invitation to the search process that ultimately brings us to new life?

1. William Stafford, "Ask Me," in *The Way It Is: New and Selected Poems* (St. Paul, MN: Graywolf Press, 1998), 56.
2. Pope Francis, *Joy of the Gospel*, par. 71.

Image 2a. Francis retires his dreams of knighthood. Statue outside of the Basilica of St. Francis. (Norberto, Il ritorno di Francesco)

Often when we think of great spiritual leaders of the past, we forget that they, too, confronted much darkness, in their own psyches as well as in the world around them, as they grew toward personal integrity and deepening relationships with God and others. In this chapter, I would like to look carefully at the early life narratives of Francis and Clare so that we can read them as mirrors into our own struggles for integrity. Their early years of doubt, confusion, and searching gradually provided them with a deep strength to say no to what was death dealing about their world. By rejecting norms and paradigms that were not providing a way toward "what better leads to God's deepening life in me,"[3] they teach us that the only way forward lies in

---

3. Our orientation to "what better leads to God's deepening life in me" and the world around me is the "Principle and Foundation" of Ignatius Loyola's *Spiritual Exercises*. See Ignatius Loyola, *Spiritual Exercises*, in *Draw Me into Your Friendship: The Spiritual Exercises, A Literal Translation and a Contemporary Reading*, ed. David L. Fleming (St. Louis: The Institute of Jesuit Sources, 1996), 27.

being deeply honest about what is not working, in our own lives and in the world around us.

Francis and Clare found this out through the rawness of their early lives. Each was propelled toward a deep search for meaning as a direct result of human violence. For Francis, it was injury during a battle against Perugian forces at Collestrada, where, at the age of twenty, he lay wounded and might have been left to die. But the Perugians recognized in Francis's suit of armor the potential value he had in captivity. Francis's experience as a prisoner of war taught him early on the double edge of wealth and power. His vulnerability during that painful year allowed him to see that, in his own ways, he had participated in the same habits of exploitation, vendetta, and violence that had left him alone and abandoned. Ransomed and returned back to his family in 1203, Francis never achieved what some today would call "successful reintegration." Rather, he began to see that continuing with business as usual was actually a slow form of death, and he grew daily more convinced that there had to be a different, better way. Clare, too, was deeply impacted by the violence embedded in both her family system and in the larger culture.

Over the course of the next two chapters, we will explore the profoundly disruptive impact that violence had in the lives of Francis and Clare as young people. This will help us to understand the urgency of their search for personal meaning, their decisive rejection of many of the norms of their culture, and their capacity to recognize early on in their lives all that is at stake in the values that our communities embody. One of their greatest contributions, both to their own contemporaries and to us today, is the depth of their desire to create a community of mutual belonging—a community in which every person matters and has a part to play in making our world a home for all. If we explore how they responded to the human hunger to belong and to be of service to something bigger than ourselves, we might discover that we, too, have similar desires. We will trace each of their stories separately, recognizing their growing influence on each other but allowing their very different backgrounds and struggles to speak independently. I would like to explore their early experience in detail, because the context of profound transition in which they lived has so many parallels to our own historical moment right now.

Pope Francis identifies our time as "a turning point in history" and asks us

> to remember that the majority of our contemporaries are barely living from day to day, with dire consequences. A number of diseases are spreading. The hearts of many people are gripped by fear and desperation, even in the so-called rich countries. The joy of living frequently fades, lack of respect for others and violence are on the rise, and inequality is increasingly evident. It is a struggle to live and, often, to live with precious little dignity. This epochal change has been set in motion by the enormous qualitative, quantitative, rapid and cumulative advances occurring in the sciences and in technology, and by their instant application in different areas of nature and of life. We are in an age of knowledge and information, which has led to new and often anonymous kinds of power.[4]

It is a system, Pope Francis states, "where the powerful feed upon the powerless," and "human beings are themselves considered consumer goods to be used and then discarded. We have created a 'disposable' culture which is now spreading," a culture of prosperity that deadens us and is sustained by the "globalization of indifference."[5] Francis and Clare remind us that we are not meant to adjust to dehumanization. We have an intuitive capacity to recognize things that, at the human level, are simply wrong and compromise our humanity. This sensitivity to pathologies within our own cultures and communities is a positive human instinct that must be cultivated for our own well-being.

Francis and Clare, too, lived in a historical moment of great turbulence and change. Small cities like theirs were the nerve centers of a massive transition from a land-based feudal economic system to the commercial revolution of the thirteenth century. Assisi is perched on a hilltop where it could be defended from external attack and where citizens, safely ensconced within the city walls, could pursue their private and collective socioeconomic interests. Assisi's success as a city

---

4. Pope Francis, *Joy of the Gospel*, par. 52.
5. Ibid., par. 53–54.

depended on the rise of the merchant class, in a painful and conflictive transition that provoked civic unrest and even war between nearby cities.

The very topography of Assisi tells this story. The Piazza del Commune is the heart of the city, and streets radiate out of it like living limbs. The piazza served as a midway point between the landholdings of the nobility and the living quarters and shops of the merchant and working classes below them. Up a steep hill east of the piazza is the church of San Rufino. Clare's noble Favarone family owned the building adjoining the church; a notarized document of 1148 shows her grandfather's pledge not to enlarge the family palace if it would interfere with the cathedral's façade. Several levels below the Favarone palace was the household of the Bernardone family.

Francis's father, Pietro di Bernardone, was a powerful and influential man, although his status was constantly shadowed by the fact that he had acquired his wealth as a cloth merchant rather than having inherited his money as a member of the noble class would have. He was a shrewd and ambitious businessman, and, as he acquired more and more wealth, he sought to purchase land in the valley below the city. In centuries past, feudal norms would have made such aspirations impossible. But times were changing. Taking advantage of many years of drought and famine toward the end of the twelfth century, Pietro bought up tracts from struggling noble families who had to liquidate their assets when the real estate failed to produce income.[6] Pietro was therefore what used to be called *nouveau riche*, and he encouraged his son Francis to spend the family's disposable income freely. Today we might call this conspicuous consumption, a practice designed to trumpet the family's growing economic power. Early sources describe Francis as being "raised to arrogance in accordance with the vanity of

6. A map of the Bernardone family's landholdings, based on Arnaldo Fortini's archival work from the early part of last century, was created for Armstrong et al., *The Saint*. However, a careful reading of the original Italian version of Fortini's biography of Francis reveals that the landholdings were likely far more extensive than the more recent map indicates. See Arnaldo Fortini, *Nova Vita di San Francesco* (Milan: Alpes, 1926), 1:101–12. According to Fortini, Francis's family's landholdings extended into Collestrada, site of the battle with the Perugians where Francis was struck down in 1202. See *Nova Vita di San Francesco*, I:103–4.

the age." Yet they are also quick to point out that even as a youth, Francis was more characterized by generosity than greed: "Since he was very rich, he was not greedy but extravagant, not a hoarder of money but a squanderer of his property, a prudent dealer but a most unreliable steward."[7] Francis appears to have been a popular young man of "charm and wit, of kindness, good humor, and the prodigal generosity of a wealthy, spoiled son" whose joyful, free spirit delighted in music and revelry of all sorts.[8]

At the age of fifteen, Francis was considered a man, able to enter apprenticeship and capable of bearing arms. He began to accompany his father on the annual trip to Troyes to learn the ins and outs of the family business. The men took goods with them to sell and purchased silk fabrics from the east that came into port cities like Genoa and Venice. Damasks, brocades, embossed silks and satin; over the years, Pietro had acquired a keen sense of market demand and was eager to teach Francis the secrets of the trade. The fair at Troyes also exposed Francis to Provençal culture—the troubadour tradition with its ideals of chivalry and courtly love—all things that he had shared with his mother in his earliest years of childhood education. The knightly ideals of this tradition fed and romanticized the exploits of war, but Francis also saw real violence in his travels—brawls, the threat of thieves on the long journey, and the need of arms to protect property. Whether on the road or in the fair's encampments, Francis could hardly have been unaware of the network of unsavory characters, ranging from thieves and moneychangers to pimps and prostitutes. Even safely home in Assisi, a great deal of violence and sexual licentiousness, often ritualized in secular and religious festivals, prevailed. Francis's privileged position enabled him to participate as he liked, squandering his wealth on frivolity that did not lack hard edges.[9]

---

7. Thomas of Celano, *Life of Saint Francis*, 1:11:2, in Armstrong et al., *The Saint*, 183, which continues: "He was, nevertheless, a rather kindly person, adaptable and quite affable, even though it made him look foolish." Cf. Bonaventure, *Life of Saint Francis*, 1:1: "The sensitivity of his gentleness, together with a refined set of manners, a patience and affability beyond human decorum, and a generosity beyond his means singled him out as a young man of flourishing natural disposition." See Armstrong et al., *The Prophet*, 531.
8. See Murray Bodo, *The Way of St. Francis: The Challenge of Franciscan Spirituality for Everyone* (New York: Image Books, 1984), 3.

Clare, on the other hand, was described universally by her peers as being one of the most upright and compassionate of Christian women, even before she entered religious life. Clare's graces and virtues consisted of her "great honesty, kindness, and humility," and witnesses at her canonization process testified repeatedly to her generosity to the poor. Not only was she described as distributing food and alms, she also tried to give away her dowry, having decided that she would not marry but would instead consecrate herself to God. Those who saw her way of life from within the cloister said just about to a person that they could not even find words to describe her holiness.[10]

Francis and Clare could hardly have come from more different social circumstances: Clare came from an influential noble household; her family's palace was located in one of the most prestigious sections of the city. Francis's family was heavily invested in overturning the traditional political dominance of the nobility in local governance. Throughout Italy, the shift from a feudal economy to a monetary based, urban economy involved massive changes in the political, social, and religious landscape. Tensions rooted in this fundamental shift in the economic base were made even more complex by the loyalties of individual cities either to the pope or to the Holy Roman Emperor. In the region of Umbria, the cities of Assisi, Rieti, Spoleto, Foligno, and Nocera were governed by Conrad I, the emperor's representative, which set them against their neighbors in Perugia, who were loyal to the papacy.[11]

The imposing Rocca Maggiore, a fortress dominating the hilltop over

---

9. Fortini's description of the grotesque "December liberties," an annual tradition lasting three weeks and full of eccentric, even sacrilegious details, is instructive in decoding Francis's later ambivalence toward his own body. See Fortini, *Nova Vita di San Francesco*, 1:98–102. Cf. Donald Spoto, *Reluctant Saint* (New York: Viking Compass, 2002) 27–35.

10. See, for example, the testimony of Benvenuta of Lady Diambra of Assisi: "The witness said that . . . she did not know how to speak of a holiness that could have been greater in her. She did not believe there had ever been another woman of greater holiness than the lady, Saint Clare, other than our Lady, the Blessed Virgin Mary." "The Eleventh Witness," 5, in *The Acts of the Process of Canonization of Clare of Assisi* in *The Lady: Clare of Assisi, Early Documents*, ed. Regis Armstrong (New York: New City Press, 2006), 182 and the testimony of Beatrice, Clare's youngest sister, who entered the convent of San Damiano in 1229 and died there in 1260, in "The Twelfth Witness," 6–7, in Armstrong, *The Lady*, 184.

11. Photographs that illustrate this material and much that follows are available under Photos at www.gillianahlgren.com.

Assisi, symbolizes the struggle.[12] In 1198, when Francis was about sixteen years old and Clare was perhaps five, the merchant class assembled an attack on Rocca Maggiore. They hoped to establish Assisi as its own commune or city state with new governing ordinances. They took advantage of a moment when Conrad was away negotiating with papal representatives, and they attacked and destroyed the residence. Francis likely participated in this attack, which successfully dismantled imperial power and established a new city government. Francis's father, Pietro, is listed in state archives as a *reipublicae benefactor et provisor*, or "financial backer and benefactor of the communal state."[13] The attempt to wrest power from the nobles of Assisi sent much of the nobility, including Clare and her family, to Perugia to seek asylum. Assisi's exiled nobles aligned themselves with the city of Perugia, a historic rival of Assisi, and together they prepared to take back the city. Four years of civil war erupted; Francis's early adulthood was marked by repeated calls to arms in battles across the Spoleto valley. Towers and fortresses were taken down; properties were trampled and destroyed. No one with landholdings in the valley could sit back and let the savage Perugian attacks go unchecked. Francis's father invested money in armor for Francis, who then prepared, with the other young men of Assisi, to go to war. Defense of the city would have been considered their civic duty, and it would have come with the blessing of the local bishop.

12. By the time of Francis's youth, it was the permanent residence of the powerful Duke of Spoleto, Conrad I, who kept a garrison of guards and hosted Emperor Henry VI when he visited. One of those notable occasions was for the baptism of Henry's son, Frederick, whose mother, Empress Constance, had unexpectedly given birth to him in Assisi, overcome by labor pains as she travelled south to meet her husband in Sicily. Francis was thirteen years old when the aging pope, Celestine III, arrived with his retinue to perform the baptism in the same font where Francis had himself been baptized. The pope's participation in the baptism of the emperor's heir was another turn in a complicated dance between papal and imperial power; the visual impression of the pope and the emperor jointly welcoming Frederick into the Christian community was a thin veneer of formality that could mask only temporarily the simmering hostilities between Perugia and Assisi. For a summary of the history of the relationship of Assisi with the Holy Roman Emperor, see Arnaldo Fortini, *Francis of Assisi*, trans. Helen Moak (New York: Crossroad, 1981), 73–84. Although Fortini's work is quite dated (and the writing style a bit romanticized), there is a wealth of helpful material there, much of which remains in the mainstream of Franciscan interpretation. Particularly informative is the material on the Assisi-Perugia conflict, city statutes pertinent to Francis (i.e., those on family law regarding inheritance and attitudes and practices toward lepers) and Francis's family's landholdings.
13. See Fortini, *Francis of Assisi*, 104.

Francis was in the elite Compagnia dei Cavalieri, when, in 1202, he was struck down and injured. His armor informed his captors of the wealth of his family and therefore saved his life; he was dragged through the streets of Perugia and thrown into prison until his family offered a suitable ransom for his return.[14] Negotiations took time, and Francis languished for nearly a year in captivity.[15] Although we know very little about this time in his life, we can easily imagine the challenges, to both body and soul, caused by confinement, injury, illness, and a host of uncertainties about his future. Being imprisoned in Perugia was deeply formative for Francis, causing him to question the social and religious values and assumptions that had led him to such ignominious circumstances.

In her own way, Clare, too, was learning how the social codes of the day prevented her from developing as a person. Ironically, throughout Francis's entire time in Perugia as a prisoner of war, Clare was also there, her family still displaced after the class struggles in Assisi. During her early years, Clare's male relatives were often absent from the household, defending the family's interests in battle and leaving domestic matters primarily in the hands of Clare's mother. In 1202, during Francis's year of imprisonment in Perugia, Clare would have been nine years old and being actively prepared for marriage and household management. She learned from her mother practical skills of reading, penmanship, and needlepoint. Yet she also observed the tremendous cost to women of the violence of the time: they were the ones to nurse the men back to health after the men were wounded in battle, and it was women who often bore the insult of sexually

---

14. No one knows for sure the site of Francis's imprisonment, but Fortini cites a nineteenth-century history of Perugia which states: "According to tradition, Francis was placed in the prisons of the Campo di Battaglia, under the site on which today stands the Palazzo del Capitano del Popolo." See Luigi Bonazzi, *Storia di Perugia dalle origini al 1860*, 2 vols. (Perugia, 1875–79), 1:261, cited in Fortini, *Francis of Assisi*, 639n84. For a summary of the sources and documentation of Francis's imprisonment, see Fortini, *Nova Vita di San Francesco*, II:169–71, 178–79.

15. The hagiographical sources are woefully silent about Francis's participation in war, his imprisonment, or any of the effects these experiences may have had on him. Thomas of Celano probably did not know of it at the time he composed the *First Life* or, for whatever reason, he chose not to incorporate the material. The first brief mention of it is contained in *The Legend of the Three Companions*, 2:4, which then becomes the source for Thomas of Celano's *The Remembrance of the Desire of a Soul*, 1:1:4.

21

transmitted diseases after the men came home. The conflicting values could not have been clearer to Clare, for her mother was devout and very committed to spiritual practices of kindness, generosity, prayer, and pilgrimages to holy places, including visits to Rome and Jerusalem. Both Francis and Clare were poised to question the assumptions of a culture of war and privilege, based on their own deeply personal observations of its cost to the human spirit.

Francis returned to Assisi dazed and disoriented after his year of imprisonment in Perugia. In taking up arms and defending his city, he had, according to all the standards of his day, made the right civic, moral, even religious decision. He had conducted himself with honor, both in battle and during his imprisonment, and yet he had suffered confinement, indignity, and the distress of not knowing when, even if, he would be released to his family. Although historical sources say almost nothing about this time in Francis's life[16]—only that he suffered grave illness—we can imagine that the dank cells, miserable food, and poor sanitation likely provoked dysentery, fever, and other disease.[17] When he finally did return to Assisi in late 1203, Francis was greatly physically weakened. His earliest biographer, Thomas of Celano, records that he was "worn down by his long illness" and hobbled about with a cane when he was finally able to get out of bed.[18] It is hard to know what these experiences did to Francis's spirit, inside and out. Certainly, they had exposed him to violence, pettiness, cruelty, callousness, and any number of indignities from which his wealth and social status had previously insulated him. His vulnerability forced him to examine and reassess the values and assumptions of his time and culture.

Before his capture, Francis looked ahead to a future that was his for the taking: successful management of his father's cloth business,

16. *The Legend of Three Companions* is the only source to provide details. See *Legend of Three Companions*, 2:4, in Regis J. Armstrong, J. A. Wayne Hellmann, and William J. Short, eds., *The Founder*, vol. 2 of *Francis of Assisi: Early Documents* (New York: New City Press, 2000), 69–70.
17. Spoto claims he contracted malaria in prison (*Reluctant Saint*, 37) while Adrian House writes: "It is possible Francis had contracted tuberculosis for he suffered from it later and wrote that he was dogged by sickness when he was young." Adrian House, *Francis of Assisi: A Revolutionary Life* (Mahwah, NJ: Paulist Press, 2001), 47.
18. Thomas of Celano, *Life of Saint Francis*, 1:2:3, in Armstrong et al., *The Saint*, 184–85.

perhaps even a celebrated marriage into a noble family—in short, a long and happy continuation of all that he had known as the cherished son of one of Assisi's notable, up-and-coming families. For a young man from a prosperous family who was accustomed to autonomy and a carefree lifestyle, imprisonment, illness, confinement, and powerlessness were radically new experiences. Alone, ill, hungry, and abused, Francis experienced a humbling vulnerability that ultimately proved invaluable to his appreciation of the holy fragility of life itself. A profound inner shift had occurred over the course of his year in Perugia, and that shift became apparent only upon his return to Assisi. Even the loving care of his mother could not restore the happy-go-lucky youth who had gone off to war. His old habits, patterns, and values ceased to hold any meaning for him. Imprisonment had shattered his casual, privileged view of life, and he found himself both unwilling and unable to return to business as usual.

* * *

We retrace this moment in Francis's life on the second day of our pilgrimage in the footsteps of Francis and Clare. The bus drops us at the top of the city of Perugia, set high on a hill, and as we head toward our first stop, the group is completely unaware that the streets we are walking on have been laid out over the city's intact medieval foundation. Like most European cities, modern Perugia was built on top of medieval Perugia, and this phenomenon is experienced in a rather exceptional way there. The labyrinth of medieval ramparts and passageways has been preserved and renovated with the inclusion of a complex set of "scala mobile," or escalators. This juxtaposition of modern and medieval is fascinating to experience in its own right, but we do this in a very special way. First we head down the streets of the modern city toward the Galleria Nazionale, where an astonishing collection of medieval Umbrian art awaits us. It is like stepping into the history of Christian art.

We spend nearly three hours contemplating the humanity of Christ as it gradually becomes more and more subtle, alive, and beautiful over the course of the centuries. We see the body of Christ on the cross taking form and shape and becoming deeply human, deeply real—no longer soaring absently over suffering, in the "Christ the victor" pose. Gradually, the body gains weight and gravity, pulled down by sin, and the self-offering of Christ becomes clearer, until finally, in a one-of-a-kind simple wooden cross that arrests your attention from across the room, Christ reaches out, leaning down toward the world with an open-armed embrace. This image is so real that, if you didn't have the curator's word for it being a mid-thirteenth-century rendition, you might wonder, as I did when I first saw it, why they had put a modern crucifix up in the middle of a room full of medieval ones. In this Cristo deposto, ostensibly an image of Christ being taken down from the cross, Christ is still caught in the pose of the cross, but his arms are not nailed. Instead they have fallen forward in a gentle, tender embrace toward the world. His eyes are closed, but even his face is tender. The outstretched arms of Christ appear in such a spontaneous, loving gesture, free from the details of suffering that appear on the other thirteenth-century crucifixes, that the contrast—like the blazing love of God itself—is almost shocking. But perhaps in this simple, piercing cross, we are given a privileged glimpse of the lens through which Francis and Clare saw Christ and saw the world: always, always through the eyes of love. We continue around the room, watching the crucifixion take on sharper dimensions, begging us, as viewers, to feel compassion, pity, sorrow, and connection.

We move onto room after room of Madonna and Child, watching their relationship come alive, Mary gradually ceasing to be a wooden-like "throne" for the miniature adult Christ on her knee and coming into herself, her humanity, her beauty, her maternity, her joy, with wonderful details of the intimacy of mother and child working their way into the images as the decades spill on. We watch their gracious affection toward one another as a real baby grasps at his mother's finger or nurses gratefully at her breast. We see the tilt of their heads toward us, the viewers, trying to draw us into the same intimacy with God and with the holy in us and in our own lives. These are the kinds of things I spend thousands and thousands of words trying to communicate in a classroom: what does it mean for us to affirm that God became truly and fully human? And the aha moment as the reality of the incarnation comes alive so clearly for people is glorious indeed. Finally, as we work our way through scene after scene, we see Francis and Clare take their place in the communion of saints, and the visual feast invites us to take more seriously, as a prayerful practice, the art of gazing and beholding, of reflection and contemplation.

It is usually about 5:00 p.m. or so when we pour, sated, out of the museum in search of a cappuccino and conversation. And even this dimension of our experience in Perugia is apropos. Perugia was known, in its time, for being a flashy city with an opulent lifestyle—full of wealth, with a propensity toward violence, both to defend its wealth and, simply, as a way of life. In our own small-scale way, we experience the careless extravagance, even hard-hearted blindness as we sit above the bowels of the city, sipping, snacking, and people watching.

But young Francis did not experience Perugia in this privileged way. The Perugians were his sworn enemies, determined to take over Assisi, and Francis rode off, innocently enough, to defend his home and his family and his people, only to be captured and imprisoned and suffer malaria and dysentery and God knows what else in the confines of prison. Everything—his dreams, his cherished ideals, his future—came tumbling down in a mass of misery there, and this becomes quite easy for us to imagine as we finish our coffees and continue our tour of the city. We descend down a long set of escalators to underneath the actual city streets, and enter a labyrinth of dark medieval passageways with gated cells on either side. We spend about twenty minutes walking in deliberate silence together, engaging in a walking meditation, pausing in front of a locked cell or two to contemplate the wretchedness that is also, so often, a hidden and repressed part of the human experience, forced down into the darkness below the superficial gaiety of the world above.

We leave Perugia with a strong sense of that fertile space that is, paradoxically, both our wounded, human vulnerability and our strength—our openness to God and to all that we trust God can and will work within us. And we reflect on the "gift of tears" described in our readings for the day—what Alan Jones, in Soul Making: The Desert Way of Spirituality, calls the tears that flow

> when the real source of our life is uncovered, when the mask of pretense is dropped, when our strategies of self-deception are abandoned. . . . To come to this place where one is truly alive, one must hit rock-bottom. There must be a breakthrough to the place of deepest helplessness. "Then at last," writes André Louf, "a beginning can be made." Tears come when we learn to live more and more

out of our deepest longings, our needs, our troubles. These must all surface and be given their rightful place. For in them we find our real human life in all its depths.[19]

*   *   *

None of Francis's early biographers mention his experience as a prisoner of war. They seem completely unaware of its impact on him. Perhaps this should not surprise us, for we are only very recently in our human history coming to terms with the long-term effects of war, on us and on our children. As the technology of war has gotten both far more sophisticated and far more sinister, we cannot afford to be naïve or self-deceptive about its impact, on us and on our world. The economic cost of war has brought about global financial and social instability as governments scramble to pay for it, and the human cost is seen in a global crisis of displacement, refugees, and cultural loss that is completely unsustainable. Surely Francis would want us to take a careful and thorough look at what has become normative in our world and to question whether or not this is what we want, for ourselves and for our children. This search for a more just, more humane way of life is precisely what he modeled for his own contemporaries after the tragedy and senselessness of war "awakened" the intense thirst of his spirit for genuine peace. Slowly, this thirst opened his eyes to a new and painful comprehension of the interlocking forces of power—economic, political, and social—that drove the violence and warfare of his day.

For Francis, the basic problem was lodged in the prevailing cultural assumption that acquiring property, and defending it when necessary, was morally neutral, even socially beneficial. This assumption bred a culture that routinely used violence when defending its economic or political interests, and church officials did nothing substantive to challenge this pattern. Bishops and popes brokered relations with political forces and then blessed young people as they went off to war in defense of economic and political interests. As the dissonances of

19. Alan Jones, *Soul Making: The Desert Way of Spirituality* (San Francisco: Harper Collins, 1989), 83.

his culture grew intolerable, Francis felt an intensifying need to say "no." No to the violence. No to the status quo. Francis's way of being creatively and courageously faithful in his day and age was not an easy way. But to him and to others it felt both necessary and freeing. This kind of honesty about what mattered to him and what moved him led to a deepening orientation to God—a God who was asking Francis to choose life, not death, for himself and for others.

As part of our walk in Francis's footsteps, perhaps we could look, for a moment, at our own world, through his eyes. Ignatius Loyola, founder of the Jesuits, would call this consideration an "examen"—an examination of conscience and consciousness—and it is a process that we engage in as we examine our own conduct and as we examine the assumptions of the communities and societies within which we live. Like Francis, Ignatius was moved toward this prayerful consideration of his life, as well as how the assumptions of his culture and society had conditioned him to see reality, as he, too, recovered from the impact of war. In many ways, Pope Francis, our first Jesuit pope, is encouraging this Ignatian practice more as an intentional, daily practice. It is in this Ignatian tradition of taking a "long, loving look at the real" that we conclude this chapter by turning from Francis's context to the historical reality of our day. But where to begin? For violence is at least as culturally, even globally, embedded in our current reality as it was in Francis's own.

We could begin by noticing the sheer scope of the problem. It might not surprise us to realize that we have grown more violent in modern times, rather than less so, and that civilians continue to suffer, in even higher numbers than active combatants. Historians estimate, for example, that in the wars of the twentieth century, not less than 62 million civilians were killed, nearly 20 million more than the 43 million military personnel killed.[20] As the technology of war has grown more sophisticated and more profitable, it has claimed more of our infrastructures, embedding its way into our global economic fabric, so that the industry of war has become nearly ubiquitous. Perhaps

20. Chris Hedges, *War is a Force that Gives Us Meaning* (New York: Public Affairs, 2002), 13.

more disturbing is how insidious war has become. What we call "the defense industry" is a powerful economic force, far surpassing the capacity of judicial systems and international organizations to monitor and intervene when human rights conventions are violated. Privatization of warfare also disrupts the relationship between combatants and the traditional civil and military codes that attempt to provide behavioral parameters or disciplinary consequences for soldiers.

War correspondent Chris Hedges has notably described war as the "force that gives us meaning." Its lethal seduction lies in its capacity to give people a cause, an identity, and a resolve that they might otherwise not be able to find on their own. In the absence of cultural, communal, and spiritual meaning, war serves as a potent and corrosive default. For the young in particular, military service can be an important source of identity: "Many of us, restless and unfulfilled, see no supreme worth in our lives. We want more out of life. And war, at least, gives us a sense that we can rise above our smallness."[21] But, as Hedges warns, engaging in warfare tends to generate a toxic culture, as war "distorts memory, corrupts language, and infects everything around it. . . . War makes the world understandable, a black and white tableau of them and us. It suspends thought, especially self-critical thought."[22] To put this another way, the social investment in violence, once war has been declared, is stronger and more pervasive than we might initially understand. Violence becomes a cultural norm and begins to displace creative alternatives within the human community. Further, once a community or nation has made a commitment to war, we tend to deny its lethal impact on all of us. Hedges comments:

> Most of us willingly accept war as long as we can fold it into a belief system that paints the ensuing suffering as necessary for a higher good, for human beings seek not only happiness but also meaning. And tragically war is sometimes the most powerful way in human society to achieve meaning.[23]

21. Ibid., 7.
22. Ibid., 3, 10.
23. Ibid.

With each technological advance, Hedges warns, "modern industrial warfare may well be leading us . . . a step closer to our own annihilation."[24] Ultimately, Hedges's own conclusions parallel those of Francis of Assisi so many centuries ago: "The only antidote to ward off self-destruction and the indiscriminate use of force is humility and, ultimately, compassion."[25] The dichotomy that Hedges articulates is one that eventually welled up within Francis, as the glamour of military victory, the spoils of war, and the prestige of knighthood evaporated, and a single, core question remained: "Whom will you serve?"

Pope Francis expresses a similar admonition to think and feel our way carefully through our circumstances and to be very careful about what we devote ourselves to. Understanding the impact of the forces in our world and their capacity to dehumanize us or annihilate us altogether emerges as one of his highest pastoral concerns. In his first apostolic letter, *Joy of the Gospel*, he writes:

> It is not the task of the Pope to offer a detailed and complete analysis of contemporary reality, but I do exhort all the communities to an "ever watchful scrutiny of the signs of the times." This is in fact a grave responsibility, since certain present realities, unless effectively dealt with, are capable of setting off processes of dehumanization which would then be hard to reverse. We need to distinguish clearly what might be a fruit of the kingdom from what runs counter to God's plan. This involves not only recognizing and discerning spirits, but also—and this is decisive —choosing movements of the spirit of good and rejecting those of the spirit of evil.[26]

If what sets humans on the pilgrim journey is a desire for meaning, then the courage to confront deception and to find our deepest truths is critical. Milan Kundera writes that the human struggle against power is the struggle of memory against forgetting. In the face of painful memories or troubling awarenesses, the temptation to forget, deny, or "move on" is even stronger. But if we are courageous enough to

24. Ibid., 13.
25. Ibid., 17.
26. Pope Francis, *Joy of the Gospel*, par. 51.

seek the truth of our lives and to press on for meaning in the face of meaninglessness, our own disillusionment can help us break through the layers of deception that surround us. Sometimes that process starts with a single question, like this one, written by a US veteran after five tours of duty in Iraq: "When the depravity of this world is laid out before you in its ruin, and you discover yourself mired in it, rather than above, what hope do you have?"[27]

War and captivity gave Francis a new critical lens through which to see the world in which he lived. Increasingly, he saw the economic, political, and cultural forces of his day—as well as the religious structures that supported and upheld them—as dispiriting and even lethal. Slowly, Francis turned what we might see as "disillusionment" into a clarion call toward a new way. The gift of these "lost years" of his life was his clarity about the brokenness of the world around him. His dissatisfaction with its message and assumptions proved to be a useful starting point for creative possibility. Francis teaches us the value of recognizing when something isn't working any more. Then humbly and collectively we can imagine something new.

27. Brian Castner, *The Long Walk: A Story of War and the Life That Follows* (New York: Anchor, 2012), 148.

3

Touched by Tenderness: Encountering God

Image 3a. The Basilica of Saint Clare and the Spoleto Valley below.

When the heart is touched by direct experience,
the mind may be challenged to change.
Personal involvement with innocent suffering,
with the injustice others suffer,
is the catalyst for solidarity
which then gives rise to intellectual inquiry and moral reflection.[1]

*   *   *

No matter where you are from, waking up for the first time in Assisi is probably not entirely like waking up at home. First, there are the birds: sparrows and larks chirping away and then, as you get up to throw open the shutters, swallows swirling around the churches, towers, and city walls, their cries of joy descending with the same elegance as they do. If, like me, you have gotten up for an early walk as the city itself is awakening, there is the delightful discovery of the daily rhythms of the townspeople: the sound of espresso grinding its way into small cups, café owners setting up their outdoor tables, merchants sweeping patios and entryways, and any number of courteous greetings as you step out to meet the day.

My mornings draw me either to the quiet of San Damiano or I get sidetracked, halfway, at the piazza Santa Chiara, where views of the gold-and-green-checked fields and valleys below Assisi invite me to pause and contemplate the olive groves, write in my journal, or listen to the nuns at the Proto-Monastery of St. Clare chant their way through matins. Each day a new beginning, each day an opportunity to meet God anew.

But where will we find this God who wants to meet us? If Assisi teaches us how to encounter God, it does so at multiple levels, especially as we try to find God through the lives of Francis and Clare. Their real stories are not quite as easy to discover or digest as we might think, and we will not meet them authentically if we are not open to profound encounter, encounter with the living God who often surprises us in unexpected places.

1. Peter-Hans Kolvenbach, "The Service of Faith and the Promotion of Justice in American Jesuit Higher Education," address at Santa Clara University, October 6, 2000, http://tinyurl.com/hwtteg2.

We come to Assisi and are struck by its beauty—the medieval walls and buildings with their rose-colored stones, the deep greens of the fields, the sounds of sheep pasturing, the riots of flowers gracing the hillside. We feel the peace and joy that are part of the residual blessing of the city's famous saints. But as we piece together the winding narratives of Francis and Clare and open our eyes to the God they came to know and cherish, we come to appreciate the complexity of encounter and the many ways that truly sharing life together will require great change of us.

*   *   *

The first step in that journey is coming to grips with how many of us belong at the expense of even more who do not. It is a recognition that the "success" of some comes on the backs of many, and that this way of life is emphatically not the kind of human flourishing that God has in mind for us. There are many who have been abandoned, many who are routinely ignored, overlooked, even despised. As Pope Francis reminds us:

> We have created a "disposable" culture which is now spreading. It is no longer simply about exploitation and oppression, but something new. Exclusion ultimately has to do with what it means to be a part of the society in which we live; those excluded are no longer society's underside or its fringes or its disenfranchised—they are no longer even a part of it.[2]

Outcast. Thrown away. Left for dead. Did Francis's experiences as a prisoner-of-war give him a new sensitivity to the disturbingly ugly reality that often exists under the glossy surface of our existence?

The way of Francis and Clare is a profound awakening to the God who walks with us, drawing us to the margins so that, slowly and steadfastly, the margins themselves are erased, and a new space, a new way is created. As Greg Boyle describes this process:

> We stand there with those whose dignity has been denied. We locate ourselves with the poor and the powerless and the voiceless. At the edges, we join the easily despised and the readily left out. We stand with the

2. Pope Francis, *Joy of the Gospel*, par. 53.

demonized so that the demonizing will stop. We situate ourselves right next to the disposable so that the day will come when we stop throwing people away. The prophet Habakkuk writes, "The vision still has its time, presses on to fulfillment and it will not disappoint . . . and if it delays, wait for it" (Hab 2:3).[3]

Francis and Clare located themselves at what Boyle calls "the edges"; they experienced a true joy in living at the margins. They demonstrate what Pope Francis has written in *Joy of the Gospel*: our joy in embodying Christ is expressed both by a concern to go to areas in greater need and to constantly go forth toward new sociocultural settings. "Wherever the need for the light and life of the Risen Christ is greatest, we will want to be there."[4] The point is to make this world a home for everyone, especially those who typically have not been included in the kinship that communicates care, safety, dignity, and worth.

Most of us start our journey for meaning from a vantage point closer to that of Francis and Clare's when they were young, prior to their conversion. Like them, we may have some awareness of God—or at least of self and other, but all of these awarenesses may not have been informed by direct connection to the God who emerges in our midst: the God who does not want our piety so much as our radical solidarity and collaboration, especially as our minds and hearts slowly take in the reality of what our brothers and sisters unjustly suffer. Conversion to this God is a slow awakening to the God who dwells in (and wants to teach us from) the spaces that seem unfit for God to inhabit.

Like Francis and Clare, we may be accustomed to looking for God in churches and other sacred places, rather than in the places of human disdain. In fact, we might find, to our chagrin, that our own habits, patterns, and assumptions (as well as those of the cultures we are part of) actually keep us from actively knowing the incarnate God, who draws us away from privilege and barriers and toward relationships that matter and change things.[5] It was Jean Vanier who said, "The

3. Gregory Boyle, *Tattoos on the Heart: The Power of Boundless Compassion* (New York: Free Press, 2010), 190.
4. See Pope Francis, *Joy of the Gospel*, par. 30.
5. Even today, most tourists who come to Assisi see a sanitized and inaccurate version of Francis, cloaked in piety but bearing little resemblance to the real story of his life. A walk around the

measure of our spirituality is our tenderness." But tenderness is not a cultural value anywhere—not even, it seems, in our religious communities. And so we must learn tenderness directly from God. Francis and Clare show us a reliable way to be sensitized to that incarnate presence.

Being touched by God can be profoundly disconcerting, even as that touch quietly teaches us what it is to be real. It brings an intimate awareness of a tenderness within ourselves, a godly tenderness that we might not ordinarily understand that we possess. We may not know what to do about such awareness, how to act upon it or with whom to share it—especially at first. But this is the ultimate brilliance of "the way that God had with me," as Francis of Assisi tries to describe his life in his last word to us, his *Testament*. It is a way that is paradoxically both dramatic and initially confusing—not easily responded to, until experiences of encounter become a way of life. Some would call this process "incarnation"—a way of life constantly sensitized to the presence of God within the human community, a recognition and affirmation of the presence of God in our midst that helps us deliberately orient ourselves to becoming the kind of human community that God wants.

Whatever we call this process matters much less than that we are deeply invested in a world in which margins are being erased because of where we choose to stand. Pope Francis describes this process when he writes that "encounter—or renewed encounter—with God's love blossoms into an enriching friendship." Through this friendship, we are liberated "from our narrowness and self-absorption" and come to know a whole new way of being human.[6]

---

upper basilica of San Francesco reveals the Giotto fresco cycle, in which there is no encounter whatsoever with the leper. Instead, Giotto, following Thomas of Celano's *Life of Saint Francis*, has substituted a story actually derived from St. Martin of Tours, of Francis giving his cloak to a poor knight. It is the closest scene to any narrative of encounter (other than Francis before the Sultan) in the entire fresco cycle. Was Francis's plea that we stay faithful to Christ the leper so challenging that no one was willing to hear or heed it?

6. See Pope Francis, *Joy of the Gospel*, par. 8.

Encounter as a Way of Life and a Transforming Process

For Francis and Clare, encounter became an arresting way of life, open to all. In their experience, there was no one whose life would not be deeply enriched by deeper dedication to the way of encounter. Engaging the other with the intention to listen, to learn, and to connect is a mutually transformative practice that slowly changes everything. Encounter teaches us to honor the fragility and sacredness of our own humanity, especially as we come to know our common humanity together. When done in the conscious presence of the love of God, encounter creates sacred space in the human community. Encounter moves us from observers of life to collaborators, with God, in the building up of the human community, the creation of a common home. Francis and Clare force us to ask ourselves what "conversion" really means, and to engage genuine conversion as a process: the quiet and precious gestation of something sacred, as we come to recognize and nurture God's tender presence, in us and in our world. Uncovering this presence is arduous; Teilhard de Chardin's helpful phrase, "the slow work of God," points to its subtlety and its sacredness.[7] Further, God's presence is made all the more fragile by the precariousness of so many, who live in circumstances of crushing poverty and horror: children sold into slavery, people routinely abused, and growing impunity for those who exploit them. The process of recognizing God's presence in our midst is as counter-cultural and even revolutionary as it is subtle, profound, and thorough. It is a revolution of tenderness that rewrites what it means to be human. And it begins with the piercing recognition of God asking us for help in the face of those who suffer injustice.

Francis and Clare's thorough commitment to the incarnate God was an ever-deepening awakening to the presence of God that each had already intuitively sensed, then actively began to seek, until finally

---

7. "Above all, trust in the slow work of God. We are, quite naturally, impatient in everything to reach the end without delay. We should like to skip the intermediate stages. We are impatient of being on the way to something unknown, something new. And yet it is the law of all progress that it is made by passing through some stages of instability—and that it may take a very long time." Pierre Teilhard de Chardin, *The Making of a Mind: Letters from a Soldier Priest, 1914–1919*, trans. René Hague (New York: Harper and Row, 1965), 57.

they deeply embraced a revolutionary way of life. Both Francis and Clare could easily identify a moment of graced action that divided their lives into a "before" and "after"—a formative time in which the shape and meaning of their lives crystallized for them. But this was emphatically not a case of life "before God" and "after God." It was more precisely a summoning invitation from the incarnate God known at the margins of society, a "wake-up call" to the presence of God in the drama of humankind, which piercingly corrected many of the inaccuracies in the religiosity of their day. They had a growing consciousness of the presence of God,[8] signaled by a dramatic coalescence of events and decisions that propelled them to create a new context in which new forms of living partnership with God—what I always call "the mystical life"—could prosper.[9]

But that mystical life had a definite starting point, in which the love of God manifested itself more clearly and particularly, eliciting a set of responses that set them on their journey.[10] As he tells us unequivocally in his *Testament*, the most definitive description of "the way God had with me," Francis first learned the power of God in one of the most frightening spaces of the medieval world: a leper colony. How did

8. For a preliminary discussion of this phrase, see Bernard McGinn, *The Foundations of Mysticism: Origins to the Fifth Century* (New York: Crossroad, 1991), xv–xx. What I find so helpful about his phrase "the consciousness of the presence of God" is that it subtly reminds us of what we often affirm verbally—that God is always present—but that we fail to live in as our reality—either our deepest reality or our more mundane, day-to-day reality. Embracing and cultivating the reality of God's presence, both in the deepest, most formative ways and in each and every daily encounter, is the fundamental brilliance of the Franciscan way of life.

9. My use of the term "mystical life" here is not intended vaguely. I would define the "mystical life" in the context of definitions developed by Bernard McGinn and others, who argue that mysticism is a way of life (as opposed to a single or even a series of particular experiences) marked by transpersonal growth, integration of reflective insights and awarenesses, and dedication to moral and spiritual integrity and human flourishing; that it consists at least as much in reflection on the meanings of the presence of God that one is increasingly made aware of as it does in whatever experiences of God one has; and that it cannot be divorced either from the context of one's historical, human experience or from religious traditions, which give us interpretive language and frameworks for seeking and forming meaning.

10. In this sense, the smaller, daily "conversions" that supported their growth in the mystical life after their formal commitment to God might be seen as "navigation," somewhat distinct from the more abrupt turns of "conversion" in the earliest years. As we seek greater intimacy with God and greater authenticity of life, we must keep navigating (steering, turning toward the movement of God in our lives) as the terrain of our humanity changes, within us and around us. By this I mean that in each moment we are called to take the sum total of wisdom that we have painstakingly acquired up to the present moment, adapt it to the next set of challenges, and temper or refine our goals and priorities, aligning them with the promptings of the Spirit as we proceed.

he get there? What led Francis to venture out into the space of the outcast?

We left Francis in the last chapter grappling with a growing awareness of his human vulnerability and with many questions about the values he had inherited from his family and his society. His return to Assisi, while a liberation from the hardships of confinement in the prison of Perugia, was not easy. He suffered, as we noted already, a "long illness," which required considerable time and attention to overcome. Medieval people lacked our contemporary psychological and medical understanding of post-combat trauma, but that lens helps us to imagine even more holistically the crisis of meaning he experienced after war and imprisonment. Perhaps an integral part of the "long illness" that then ate at him was the challenge of reflecting on the worth and value of his life up to this point and feeling that he had done nothing that was lasting, meaningful, or significant. "Is this really all there is?" Forced, first in the prison cell in Perugia and then on the sickbed in Assisi, to try to make peace with his heart, perhaps Francis intuitively sensed that turning discontent into such a task was not only possible but might be the only way to true happiness.

The steps of conversion that unfold after Francis's imprisonment stem, ultimately, from this inner stirring, a divine restlessness that stimulates the desire to make one's home in two simultaneous places: the deep mystery of one's own heart, nurturing a relationship with the God who is found there, and the world around us, which challenges us to find God in the ordinary, in the messiness, in the suffering, and in the joy that we find as we share life together. As we reconstruct the elements of this process, we can see that the crucified Christ, who reflects so absolutely the love of God-with-us, could speak to Francis so powerfully from the cross of San Damiano because, by then, Francis himself had already been pierced and wounded, body and soul, by the darkness of humanity. Thus, the prayer of Francis's heart, his soul instinct, was to seek true light and love despite and perhaps even within the reality of his humanity. And what propels him forward in a quest toward deeper integrity and purity of heart is a recognition and growing acceptance of his own brokenness, his incompletion, and the inner hunger of his heart for wholeness.

We can say that Francis's prison cell in Perugia provided the first real occasion for Francis to engage the space where his heart and the complexities of the world around him came together—ironically, a place of brokenness in which he was surrounded by shattered dreams, unanswered questions, and his own undeveloped potential. Staying with that brokenness—being honest about it and coming to terms with it—allowed him slowly to explore his natural capacities of empathic understanding, solidarity with others, compassion, and cultivating loving relationships, and put them to use in the service of God and others. All of this would take time and patience to unfold. But Francis's time in Perugia left him unable to return to his life of aggressive and conspicuous consumption, which now held all the appeal of shards of broken glass. Slowly, Francis found his former dreams far too small. Although he had, as yet, no other dreams to replace them, he was, at least, honest about the profound discontent he felt as daily life ceased to have any real meaning for him.

Francis's mother, Pica, appears to have had much greater patience with Francis's recovery process than his father, Pietro, who expected Francis to reengage in the family's luxury cloth business without further delay. But dreams die hard. Restless and unwilling to settle into his father's life, Francis conceived another plan. While in prison, he had heard from a knight of Apulia about the bravery of Gautier de Brienne, a Frenchman in the service of the pope, who had routed the German imperial troops. When another young man in Assisi, already of the noble class, spoke of his intention to join Gautier on crusade, Francis decided to go along and try to earn a knighthood. Apulia was about two hundred miles southeast of Assisi. Francis got no farther than the town of Spoleto when he decided to turn back and return home. What exactly happened on that journey is unclear, although it was definitive.

Thomas of Celano, one of Francis's early hagiographers, describes how a dream communicated to Francis that God was asking of him a different type of service than that of knighthood.[11] Our deeper contemporary understanding of post-traumatic stress disorder and the symptoms that can be triggered when our current circumstances approximate spaces of previous trauma give us another way of understanding this pivotal moment. In any case, Francis's dream of knighthood evaporated forever. He returned to Assisi in the fall of 1205 only to face new suspicions from his father that he was a coward and a failure. The pressure to prove his worth intensified.

After his dream of military glory faded away, Francis's inner restlessness took on greater dimensions. Thomas of Celano describes him at this time:

> He prayed with all his heart that the eternal and true God guide his way and teach him to do His will. He endured great suffering in his soul, and he was not able to rest until he accomplished in action what he had conceived in his heart. . . . He was burning inwardly with a divine fire, and he was unable to conceal outwardly the flame kindled in his soul. . . . While his past and present transgressions no longer delighted him, he was not yet fully confident of refraining from future ones.[12]

A simple prayer coming from his humble spirit epitomizes this searing time in his life:

Most High,
all-glorious God,
enlighten the darkness of my heart.
Give me
true faith,
certain hope,
and perfect love,

11. Celano describes a dream in which Francis saw a castle full of spacious rooms full of arms and military weapons promising glory and was asked to choose between that glory and the service of God. See Thomas of Celano, *Remembrance of the Desire*, 1:2:6, in Armstrong et al., *The Founder*, 245: "As he slept one night, someone spoke to him a second time in a vision and asked with concern where he was going. He explained his plan and said he was going to Apulia to become a knight. The other questioned him anxiously 'Who can do more for you, the servant or the lord?' 'The lord!' said Francis. 'Then why do you seek the servant instead of the lord?' Francis then asked: 'Lord, what do you want me to do?' And the Lord said to him: 'Go back to the land of your birth because I will fulfill your dream in a spiritual way.' He turned back without delay." This scene is not included in Thomas of Celano's *Life of Saint Francis*. Because the dream was depicted by Giotto on the famous frescoes of the basilica of San Francesco as an integral part of Francis's early conversion experience, it has remained in the popular imagination.
12. Thomas of Celano, *Life of Saint Francis*, 1:3:6, in Armstrong et al., *The Saint*, 187.

sense and understanding,
Lord,
that I may know and do
Your holy and true command.[13]

By the end of 1206, two major events provided Francis with a greater sense of direction; these events signal the convergence of a new orientation within him, one that would cause him to make a radical break with all that he had previously known. They are described in every biography of Francis, from the earliest to the most recent: Francis's encounter with the leper and his attraction to the ruined church of San Damiano, whose crucifix became a focal point of Franciscan prayer. Not only do these events form the crux of Francis's inner experience of a living God, they also solidify and shape his external commitments for the rest of his life. While they are distinct events, they are best understood in relationship to one another, as compelling communications from an incarnate God vividly demanding his attention.[14] Solidarity with the suffering body of Christ, especially

13. Armstrong et al., *The Saint*, 40. The prayer is found in *The Legend of the Three Companions*, several manuscripts of which say that it was uttered in response to the crucifix he discovered in a dilapidated church called San Damiano outside the city walls of Assisi, a church that would soon become the very heart of his new life, although he did not yet know it. If so, the prayer would be dated about 1206/7. The precise timing seems less important, for it is likely that Francis prayed this prayer or one like it daily as a simple form of self-offering and an affirmation of his radical openness to God during this period of search and struggle.

14. In fact, of these two events, Francis himself describes only the encounter with the leper as being formative. Neither Thomas of Celano's *Life of Saint Francis* (though it specifically mentions the church of San Damiano, which was "threatening to collapse because of age") nor Julian of Speyer's *Life of Saint Francis* recounts an experience of Francis actually hearing the words "Francis, rebuild my home" from the crucifix. However, the theme of "rebuilding God's home"—that is, both in the physical sense of rebuilding the church of San Damiano (as well as two other churches in the valley below Assisi) and the metaphorical sense of reforming the contemporary Christian community in light of the gospel—is a critical part of the Franciscan tradition. The event of the crucifix actually speaking to Francis is first contained in the *Legend of the Three Companions*, 5:13, in Armstrong et al., *The Founder*, 76: "While he was walking by the church of San Damiano, he was told in the Spirit to go inside for a prayer. Once he entered, he began to pray intensely before an image of the Crucified, which spoke to him in a tender and kind voice: 'Francis, don't you see that my house is being destroyed? Go, then, and rebuild it for me.'" Thomas of Celano incorporates the story into his *Remembrance of the Desire*, 1:6:10 (Armstrong et al., *The Founder*, 249): "The image of Christ crucified spoke to him. 'Francis,' it said, calling him by name, 'go rebuild My house; as you see, it is all being destroyed.'" Giotto's frescoes and Bonaventure's *Life of St. Francis* enshrine this episode into the popular consciousness of Francis, even though it is likely far more symbolic than literal. Jacques Dalarun summarizes this legendary tradition and concludes that, "Although it has no historical basis, it will later be one of the episodes most used in preaching in the second half of the thirteenth century." Dalarun recognizes the narrative's symbolic value to express "the destiny of the saint and the destiny of the Order." See Jacques Dalarun, *The Misadventures of Francis*

41

as it is known at the margins of society, gradually became, for Francis, the way into a whole new form of life.

In his own account of this period in his life, described in the *Testament* he wrote shortly before his death, Francis tells us that being drawn into the leper colony and the flood of feelings that overcame him once there was, for him, a singular expression of God's compassionate and tender love. Although we can and should speak of this experience as one of radical tenderness, it was not a "Hallmark moment." This was an experience of being pulled, immediately, out of his malaise and despair, of knowing a depth of connection that overcame him, of feeling a quickening of life flowing through him that now sought to extend itself into solidarity with people who had always horrified him. All of this showed Francis, instantly and directly, both who God was and who God called him to be.

Despised by society and condemned to a miserable life in colonies outside the city walls, lepers were absolutely dependent upon those few who dared to share the same bleak fate that they did. The radical ostracism of lepers in medieval society is hard to exaggerate. Francis's first real encounter with them in 1206 was hardly the first time he became aware of them. There were several leper colonies in the Spoleto valley, and Francis traveled through the valley often, whether on business or pleasure.[15] But these colonies were places that Francis (and everyone, for that matter) always purposely avoided. Early sources record how "he used to hold his nose, not only when he saw lepers themselves nearby, but even their homes at a distance"[16] and that "he used to say that the sight of lepers was so bitter to him that in the days of his vanity when he saw their houses even two miles away, he would cover his nose with his hands."[17] Francis's horror and disgust at the disease, in which flesh grew infected and putrefied

of Assisi: Toward a Historical Use of the Franciscan Legends, trans. Edward Hagman (St. Bonaventure, NY: Franciscan Institute Publications, 2002), 200.

15. San Lazaro (later named La Maddalena) was the leper colony of greatest importance to Francis. Other communities in the area include San Rufino dell'Arce near the Portiuncula and the colony of San Salvatore delle Mura, at the present day Casa Gualdi.
16. Julian of Speyer, *Life of Saint Francis*, 2:12, in Armstrong et al., *The Saint*, 377.
17. Thomas of Celano, *Life of Saint Francis*, 1:7:17, in Armstrong et al., *The Saint*, 195.

until extremities rotted, was shared by all his contemporaries, who vigorously worked together to exclude lepers from any part of civil society. Even the church turned its back on them completely. Strict statutes were in place to keep lepers from entering the city walls or appealing in any way to Christian conscience: "No leper may dare to enter the city or walk around in it, and if any one of them shall be found, everyone may strike him with impunity."[18]

Leprosy was a wretched and painful condition, but the suffering that lepers endured was more than simply physical. It was emotional, relational, and social. Lepers could neither work nor maintain contact with their families, and they had no identity beyond that of "leper." Their clothing, begging bowl, clapper, and warning bell set them apart from the world, and the leper colony was a place of extreme deprivation, even unto death. A ritual similar to a funeral rite greeted those condemned to the leper colony; to walk into one was a permanent sentence to a slow and painful death. No wonder Francis shuddered at the thought of the leper colony. It was not just disgust at the physical condition, it was also horror at the absolute helplessness and vulnerability of people there, many of whom could neither feed nor clothe themselves. No "self-respecting" person in Francis's society could or would associate with these untouchables.

Because Francis knew that it was beyond his ability to even want to reach out to them, it was easy for him to recognize the tenderness[19] [*misericordia*] he felt for them as an act of God, a profound infusion of God's own love in his heart. As he describes his moment of conversion in the leper colony:

> The Lord gave me, Brother Francis, thus to begin doing penance in this way: for when I was in sin, it seemed too bitter for me to see lepers. But then God Godself led me among them and I showed loving kindness

---

18. Fortini, *Francis of Assisi*, 211. These statutes were not specific to Assisi. All cities had them and many extended penalties to those who associated with lepers. In Perugia, for example, a statute of 1279 condemned women who had sexual relationships with lepers to be flogged through the cities and suburbs, have their noses cut off, and be banished permanently from the city.
19. I am using the word "tenderness" here interchangeably with the word "*misericordia*," best translated as loving kindness. This word and its meaning will be developed further in the next chapter.

[*misericordia*] to them. And when I left them, what had seemed bitter to me was turned into sweetness of soul and body.

The experience was enough to change him forever, as he tells us, "And afterwards I delayed a little but then I left the world."[20]

The stunning experience of finding God in what was, for Francis, the most unexpected and unimaginable place—a place of horror and suffering—must have been profoundly disconcerting. And yet to have found love, connection, passion, and even joy in a place that he expected to feel disgust was also compelling.

As Francis began to accept vulnerability as an integral element of his own humanity, he found he had much to learn from those who lived with the pain of feeling rejected, ignored, and alone. For several years, he had known that something profound was missing from his life: now the joy and fellowship he found with those left for dead gave him a new clue as to how to find meaning in his own life. Francis's initial experience at the leper colony taught him what he already instinctively knew: "The joy of life comes from the ways in which we live together and the pain of life comes from the many ways we fail to do that well."[21]

20. Francis of Assisi, *Testament*, in Armstrong et al., *The Saint*, 124. Fortini argues that this particular encounter took place at the leper colony of San Lazaro, renamed La Maddalena after Mary Magdalene in the fourteenth century.
21. While on pilgrimage, in our reflections on this time in Francis's life, we often use this passage from Henri Nouwen's *Life of the Beloved* in which he discusses the human experience of brokenness. "There are many things I would like to say to you about our brokenness. But where to begin? Perhaps the simplest beginning would be to say that our brokenness reveals something about who we are. Our sufferings and pains are not simply bothersome interruptions of our lives; rather, they touch us in our uniqueness and our most intimate individuality. The way I am broken tells you something unique about me. The way you are broken tells me something unique about you. This is the reason for my feeling privileged when you freely share some of your deep pain with me, and that is why it is an expression of my trust in you when I disclose to you something of my vulnerable side." As is commonly known, Henri Nouwen, a Roman Catholic priest and professor of spirituality at Yale Divinity School, found a spiritual and physical home within the L'Arche community, a movement started by Jean Vanier that blended profoundly disabled adults with others in intentional Christian community. His reflections on the challenges faced by some in his community are particularly helpful to our understanding of what the experience of a medieval leper might have felt like: "In my own community, with many severely handicapped men and women, the greatest source of suffering is not the handicap itself, but the accompanying feelings of being useless, worthless, unappreciated, and unloved. It is much easier to accept the inability to speak, walk, or feed oneself than it is to accept the inability to be of special value to another person. We human beings can suffer immense deprivations with great steadfastness, but when we sense that we no longer have anything to offer to anyone, we quickly lose our grip on life. Instinctively, we know that the joy of life comes from the ways in which we live together and that

While on pilgrimage, we read a passage that, for me, captures the essence of this wounding yet liberating moment for Francis. It is from Alan Jones's *Soul Making: The Way of Desert Spirituality*:

> Christianity is a shocking religion, although many of its adherents have managed to protect themselves from its terrible impact. . . . It claims that the flesh matters. It insists that history (the particularity of time and place) matters. Above all it claims that, in the end, nothing else but love matters. Much of the discipline of the spiritual life is concerned with keeping the shock and promise of love alive. Without the occasional abrasive brush with the unexpected, human life soon becomes a mere matter of routine; and, before we know where we are, a casual indifference and even brutality takes over and we begin to die inside. The shock breaks open the deadly "everydayness" that ensnares us and brings something awesome and terrifying to our reluctant attention; the believer's name for that "something" is God. God ceases to be a subject for philosophical debate, still less the object of our part-time and casual allegiance. This God is no hobby. God is felt in places too deep for words; . . . God is felt in pain, sorrow, and contradiction. This, in itself, comes as a shock, since we tend to make religion only of our better moments. . . . One of the ways that the shock of Christ is kept alive is by means of "compunction," a kind of "puncturing" of the heart. Compunction is the word for that which pierces us to the heart, cuts us to the quick, raises us from the "dead." Compunction administers the shock that is necessary for us to be who we really are—to wake up to our reality and our deepest truth. . . . The will is liberated for action.[22]

This description captures, I think, some of what Francis felt upon leaving the leper colony for the first time. He had been "pierced" by a God felt in a place too deep for words. Looking back up the hill to Assisi, mustn't he have wondered where he really belonged?

the pain of life comes from the many ways we fail to do that well." Henri Nouwen, *Life of the Beloved* (New York: Crossroad, 1992), 89–90.
22. Alan Jones, *Soul Making*, 84–85.

Image 3b. View of Assisi from the valley below.

When I take groups down to the former leper colony in the valley outside of Assisi, I often imagine the moment when Francis left that leper colony for the first time. His heart has been turned inside out; he knows something definitive has just happened to him. Something has now validated his discontent, this growing instinct driving him to question his life, its meaning, and all of the goals that have been imposed upon him by his family and his society. Now the hollowness of all that he himself has willingly and anxiously embraced is suddenly exposed for what it is. Forlornly, he looks back up the hillside to the city that has been home for him all of his life, that he has given his life and health to defend. Slowly he realizes that he is, in reality, just as homeless as the lepers who have shown him his own heart and have given him access to the very heart of God. Although it is still a deep and shocking mystery to him, he senses that down here in the exposed plain of the valley, amidst those with nowhere else to go, he has finally found his home and a new and ultimate purpose for his life: to work with others to make the world a home for all.

From Encounter to Solidarity

Scholars who might disagree about how to interpret other elements of Francis's experience converge in noticing that his first encounter with God in the leper colony is key to understanding the rest of Francis's life. Many identify this moment as an essential experience of grace; it was the divine spark capable of igniting the revolution of tenderness to which Francis would dedicate himself. The encounter gave Francis insight into the very nature of God; in effect, it was, for him, a radical communication of God's own aliveness. In the leper colony, Francis discovered the living God. And in response, he devoted himself to continually deepening his relationship with the God who comes alive in loving encounter.

When Pope Francis speaks of creating a culture of encounter capable of changing the culture of indifference and exclusion, it is this kind of encounter that he means. For through encounter with God in those who were traditionally excluded and cast out of society, Francis learned the fundamental characteristics of God: compassionate, ever-abundant love and life-giving presence. Additionally, he saw that these fundamental characteristics of God came together in and through the incarnation—that is, the presence of God as experienced and mediated within humanity. The promise in scripture that "where two or three are gathered in my name, I will be with you" was made real for him in that moment. Encounter is, then, sacramental, incarnational, very real, very human, and very sacred, all at once.

Francis had discovered, to his surprise, that God could be known, experienced, revered, and nurtured in the human community, and it was the poor and disenfranchised lepers who had shown this to him.[23] The coldness and superficiality of his own lifestyle were laid bare as he realized that, when it came to love, he had a great deal to learn from people he never expected could teach him anything. In the leper colony, Francis discovered a whole new way of experiencing the body

---

23. The importance of being shown the way into God through the marginalized is reinforced in the form of life that Francis eventually drew up for his companions, where living in a leper colony was an integral part of the novitiate, or time of initial formation of the early Franciscans.

of Christ, whose presence was known in *communio,* the shared union of God savored and enjoyed in community. Finding and sustaining that joy in community, as a living witness to the presence of God in the mystery of human relatedness, became a critical element of the new life to which Francis felt called. Increasingly, he doubted that such a life was possible within the city walls.

Still unsure about how to respond to these inner movements and where, exactly, to locate that response, Francis was drawn to a dilapidated church, also outside the city walls, not far from the leper colonies in the valley below: the church of San Damiano. It is here that he was said to have understood the voice of God to say to him: "Francis, go and rebuild my home. Don't you see it's in ruins?" Rebuilding the church of San Damiano stone by stone became, for Francis, a concrete way to place himself in God's service, and the task of working thoughtfully with his hands gave him time to sort through his sense of God's invitation to him. Relieved to find something he could now actually do, Francis rode out to the neighboring town of Foligno to sell some of his family's cloth and a horse,[24] returning to San Damiano with a monetary offering to the priest living there. Sources say that the priest, fearing reprisal from Francis's father, refused to accept the money, although he allowed Francis to stay there.

Francis's disappearance from the family home and business did indeed attract the ire of his father, Pietro, who, by this point, found his son's behavior inexplicable. Pietro apparently believed that only discipline, punishment, and confinement would bring Francis back to his senses. Thomas of Celano describes:

> The report of these things reached the ears of many, finally reaching his father. When he heard the name of his own son mentioned and that the commotion among the townspeople swirled around him, he immediately arose . . . to destroy him. With no restraint, he pounced on Francis like a wolf on a lamb and, glaring at him fiercely and savagely, he grabbed him and shamelessly dragged him home. With no pity, he shut him up for

---

24. See Thomas of Celano, *Life of Saint Francis,* 1:4:8, in Armstrong et al., *The Saint,* 188–89. This is an errand Francis would have done many, many times for his father—but, of course, he would have returned the money collected back to the family business.

several days in a dark place. Striving to bend Francis' will to his own, he badgered him, beat him, and bound him.[25]

After business drew Pietro from the house, Francis's mother, Pica, released him from confinement. Francis returned to San Damiano to continue to make good on his promise to God. Increasingly, Francis sensed that the work of creating a hospitable space, for God and for others, was his calling and the only thing truly worth doing. But this new way of life would require a definitive break from his father, from his friends and family, and from all of the social, cultural, and religious assumptions of his day and age. The confrontation was not long in coming.

Returning from his business trip, despairing of Francis's sanity, and fearing for the financial stability of his entire life's work, Pietro formally requested a court hearing to have Francis punished.[26] There was a civil protocol for this; in order to protect the family fortune, parents could have their offspring banished from the city on the grounds of parental disobedience.[27] Pietro's case came before the civil judge in early 1207, and, when a messenger arrived at San Damiano to serve Francis with his summons, Francis claimed exemption from civil law because he was now working in the service of the church.[28] The consuls referred Pietro to the bishop. The sources converge on

---

25. Ibid., 191–92.
26. Thomas of Celano recounts: "When the father saw that he could not recall [Francis] from the journey he had begun, he became obsessed with recovering the money. . . . He led the son to the bishop of the city to make him renounce into the bishop's hands all rights of inheritance and return everything that he had. Not only did [Francis] not refuse this, but he hastened joyfully and eagerly to do what was demanded." Ibid., 193. Arguing from documents in the state archives, however, Arnaldo Fortini gives us a different view. "Given the nature of Pietro's accusations, the course he followed, and the criminal nature of the acts of dissipation of which he accused Francis, it is clear that he was not simply demanding restitution of the money but was bringing formal criminal charges against his son. The steps that he took are those outlined in the [civil] statutes for bringing criminal proceedings, and the course followed by the consuls as reflected in the ancient biographies is exactly that set by the statutes for these. Pietro could not have been simply asking the consuls to settle a bitter family quarrel, for statutes prohibited the authorities from intervening in purely family disputes unless loss of life or of limb were involved." Fortini, *Francis of Assisi*, 223.
27. For example: "The son who does not give obedience to his father and to his mother, at their request is to be banished from the city and from the district, and no one may give him anything to eat or to drink or help him in any way." In another section, guilty sons could be "imprisoned at the request of two near relatives" and they "may not be released until such time as it would please these members of their family." See Fortini, *Francis of Assisi*, 224–25.
28. A bull of Innocent III, issued in 1198, declared that any civil proceedings against a priest or anyone

this dramatic event: pleading his case before Bishop Guido outside the bishop's residence, Pietro demanded the return of the money from the sale of the cloth and the horse in Foligno. In response, Francis not only gave it to him, but stripped himself of his fine clothing, standing naked before all and handing everything back to his father. In one fell blow, he had renounced his inheritance, his status in society, and his identity as the son of Pietro di Bernardone, choosing instead "nakedly to follow the naked Christ."[29] The bishop, understanding Francis's dramatic gesture as a godly impulse toward a holier imitation of Christ, intervened by covering Francis's nakedness with his own ecclesiastical robe, signifying his endorsement of Francis's self-offering.[30] In that moment, Francis left behind not only his family but all social structures, choosing instead to forge a new identity rooted solely in the most authentic imitation of Christ and the gospel way that he could imagine.

How are we today to understand this act? Franciscan Murray Bodo argues that Francis's decision was a deeply personal one. He writes:

> I do not think that Francis was a social reformer who saw what money would do to the fabric of society. He was rather the quintessential Christian who saw what money would do to the spirit. . . . The compulsive pursuit of money, more than anything else, distracts the individual from what really brings life. And it is what happens at the core of the individual which ultimately determines what society will become.[31]

I agree that Francis's decision was deeply personal, and yet it was neither merely personal nor merely "spiritual." It was deeply *human*, and, as such, it entailed the whole of his personhood, in an action

"living in the lands of the Episcopacy" had to obtain the consent of the pope. See discussion in Fortini, *Francis of Assisi*, 225–26.

29. The reference to the naked Christ is from a letter of St. Jerome, well known in the medieval church. Without citing it directly, Bonaventure suggests it in his *Life of St. Francis*, when he concludes his description of this moment of Francis's life with: "Thus the servant of the Most High King was left naked so that he might follow his naked crucified Lord, whom he loved." Bonaventure, *Life of St. Francis*, 2:4.

30. "The bishop, observing his frame of mind and admiring his fervor and determination, got up and, gathering him in his own arms, covered him with the mantle he was wearing. He clearly understood that this was prompted by God and he knew that the action of the man of God, which he had personally observed, contained a mystery. After this he became his helper. Cherishing and comforting him, he embraced him in the depths of charity." Thomas of Celano, *Life of Saint Francis*, 1:6:15, in Armstrong et al., *The Saint*, 193–94.

31. See Bodo, *Way of St. Francis*, 21.

that was both personal and relational. It was Francis's humanity that was being compromised by the political, economic, social, and religious structures. And they compromised others as much as they compromised him. It was commonly assumed that people would willingly adopt a contemptuous stance toward those who lived in the leper colony, who begged for a living, or who otherwise lived in the margins of society. In understanding the cost of such contempt for others to his humanity (not just his soul), Francis was making a compelling case for the need to free ourselves from anything that debases us. I think of this as a personal statement as well as a statement to the whole human community, almost like saying: "Our way of life so compromises my integrity that I must disidentify myself from it. I may not know exactly who I am being called to become, but I do know that I cannot become who I must without setting off upon an entirely different way."

It is neither too stark nor too simplistic to understand that Francis's encounters at the margins were revealing inconsistencies in his life and culture, and they now made certain demands of him. They required him to say no to forces in his society and culture that diminished human dignity and asked him to choose instead toward a new and "wonderfully complicated" way of being connected to others. Pope Francis captures this invitation to reclaim our humanity in *The Joy of the Gospel* when he writes:

> Sometimes we are tempted to be that kind of Christian who keeps the Lord's wounds at arm's length. Yet Jesus wants us to touch human misery, to touch the suffering flesh of others. He hopes that we will stop looking for those personal or communal niches which shelter us from the maelstrom of human misfortune and instead enter into the reality of other people's lives and know the power of tenderness. Whenever we do so, our lives become wonderfully complicated and we experience intensely what it is to be a people, to be part of a people.[32]

Like Francis so many centuries ago, Pope Francis writes, we are being called to the same kind of "ever watchful scrutiny of the times," so

---

32. Pope Francis, *Joy of the Gospel*, par. 270.

that, with a similar clarity of vision, we can say no to an economy of exclusion and inequality,[33] to "the dictatorship of an impersonal economy lacking a truly human purpose" and the tyranny of a consumption that "unilaterally and relentlessly imposes its own laws and rules."[34] As Francis of Assisi saw so clearly, "an evil embedded in the structures of a society has a constant potential for disintegration and death. It is an evil crystallized in unjust social structures, which cannot be the basis of hope for a better future."[35]

In turning his back upon dehumanizing political, economic, social, and religious structures, Francis freed himself to explore a new way of being human. Although he did not set out to start a new movement, I think that it quickly became clear to him that he would make little real progress on this way alone. Francis had been drawn into a new kind of personhood through the community of lepers down in the valley. Now taking the cloak of a beggar, Francis began to live outside the city walls with lepers and outcasts, completing the reconstruction of San Damiano and beginning to receive people there to live together in poverty, simplicity, and service. As the fledgling community grew, its affiliates began to restore other churches in the area, including the church of Santa Maria degli Angeli on a small portion of land in the valley known as the Portiuncula. And at this moment, Francis's life narrative and Clare's began to converge.

While Clare was not likely present at Francis's dramatic self-stripping in the courtyard outside the bishop's palace, she surely knew of it.[36] The changes in his behavior and the escalating confrontation between Francis and his father had been fodder for public gossip, which would have reached her in one form or another. But Clare would likely have had a very different interpretation of Francis's growing estrangement with the sociopolitical world of Assisi than most of her friends and family. In fact, she was quite sensitive, from her own lived

33. See Ibid., par. 53–54.
34. Ibid., par. 55–56.
35. Ibid., par. 59.
36. Clare and her family would have returned to Assisi from Perugia perhaps around 1205, as hostilities between the two cities began to ebb. See Fortini, *Francis of Assisi*, 166–69.

experience, to the same tensions with which Francis struggled. She saw, as he did, that the predominant social, economic, political, and even religious norms of their day, whether experienced as a member of the noble or merchant class, were not conducive to the simplicity of the gospel. In her own way, Clare was as cognizant as Francis was of the deep and inherent compromises that success in their sociopolitical spheres and family circles entailed. Owning property meant defending property—and the cost of this was dear. As Joan Mueller cogently notes:

> Clare and Francis had both grown up with and experienced firsthand the consequences of violence, riots, ambushes, and battles. Their families had grown rich off the backs of the poor. The youth of Assisi was losing heart with the constant struggle to have more and more. While the appetite of their fathers was insatiable, the sons and daughters of Assisi seemed to be sickened by the very thought of continuing the gluttonous struggle to acquire more. . . . This social context makes Francis's and Clare's choice of poverty understandable. In an era when families fought families, and churchmen and monastics were entering into litigation to protect and expand wealth, Assisi's children saw that they had no future if they continued the behavior of their parents. If Francis had taken the way of his father, he probably would have died on a battlefield without singing for the world his *Canticle of Creation*. If Clare had not run away from the prison of her noble palazzo, she might have ended her days as a widow grieving over her husband and sons who died on some field for a senseless purpose. Instead, Francis, the merchant, and Clare, the noblewoman, made another choice. They called their choice "poverty."[37]

And yet, what others saw as poverty and renunciation, Francis and Clare knew to be freedom and integrity.[38]

Their collaboration started early; Clare would have been only about fifteen years old.[39] From the testimony of her family members and

---

37. Joan Mueller, trans., *Clare of Assisi: The Letters to Agnes* (Collegeville, MN: Liturgical Press, 2003), xiv–xv.
38. An early document, *The Anonymous of Perugia*, describes an exchange between Francis and the local bishop in which Francis states this clearly: "One day when the blessed Francis had gone to that bishop, the bishop told him: 'It seems to me that your life is very rough and hard, not having or possessing anything in this world.' The saint of God answered: 'Lord, if we had any possessions, we would need arms to protect them because they cause many disputes and lawsuits. And possessions usually impede the love of God and neighbor. Therefore we do not want to possess anything in this world.' And this answer pleased the bishop." *Anonymous of Perugia*, 5:17, in Armstrong et al., *The Founder*, 41.

early friends gathered prior to her canonization, we know that Clare had made a habit of giving to the poor out of her portion of the household purse. As Francis continued his work of restoring churches outside the city walls (we are in the year 1208 now, more or less[40]), Clare showed her solidarity with him by sending money down to those working on the Portiuncula to sustain them.[41] As she came of age, her financial support grew, extending into her dowry and even a portion of her sister's.[42]

As Francis began to engage more actively in preaching, he returned to the piazza outside the church of San Giorgio, where he had been educated as a boy, and also to the piazza San Rufino just outside Clare's house, where she would have heard his words. Francis's preaching and the simplicity of his life were already attracting others willing to give up their wealth and social position, just as Francis had. One of the earliest of these was a wealthy, educated nobleman named Bernardo di Quintavalle, whose dedication to poverty must have caused as much public scandal as Francis's had. Bernardo had degrees in both civil and canon law, and he was much respected around the city. After consulting with Francis, he liquidated his extensive assets, including land on the hill and in the valley below Assisi, olive groves, and vineyards. All the proceeds were given away to the poor. Joined by another doctor of law, Peter of Catanio, and one of Clare's own cousins, Rufino, the group settled into the Portiuncula. By the fall of 1209, when Francis and his companions numbered eight, they decided to leave Assisi on a lengthy preaching tour; according to Thomas of Celano, two of them went as far as Santiago de Compostela in northwestern Spain.[43]

---

39. Rather than thinking of Clare as Francis's "spiritual daughter," as Donald Spoto calls her, we should understand her as a patron and, increasingly, a partner in the work of reform and ministry that Francis engaged.

40. Thomas of Celano records that the reconstruction of the church of the Portiuncula took place "in the third year of his conversion. At this time [Francis] wore a sort of hermit's habit with a leather belt. He carried a staff in his hand and wore shoes." Thomas of Celano, *Life of Saint Francis*, 1:9:21, in Armstrong et al., *The Saint*, 201. Shortly thereafter, Francis heard the gospel text that caused him to move into deeper expressions of poverty.

41. See the testimony of Lady Bona of Guelfuccio: "The Seventeenth Witness," in *Acts of the Process of Canonization*, par. 7, in Armstrong, *The Lady*, 193.

42. See testimony of Clare's sister Beatrice, below, p. 60.

43. See Thomas of Celano, *Life of Saint Francis*, 1:12:30, in Armstrong et al., *The Saint*, 207. For a more

Francis was living his dream of the gospel life, practicing as precise an imitation of Christ as he knew.

But leaving the confines (and jurisdiction) of the Spoleto valley required more ecclesiastical support than the bishop of Assisi could give them. As Francis's revolutionary way of life began to catch on, it attracted attention, notoriety, and the possibility of resistance on many fronts. In 1209 or 1210, Francis wrote out a simple, gospel-based way of life, and went with his brothers down to Rome to seek papal approval of this new way.[44] The encounter of Francis with Pope Innocent III deserves some consideration, particularly because commentators often use the event to demonstrate either Francis's "uniqueness" (in other words, so the argument runs, he must have been recognizably different from his contemporaries in order to have so easily received papal approval) or a strong urge toward orthodoxy and obedience. Neither of these views captures either the encounter or its significance.

First, it is clear that Francis was hardly unique in his desire to embrace the gospel life. Nor was he unique for his ability to forge a positive working relationship with this particular pope. A formal relationship with the church universal was necessary if Francis's gospel way of life was truly going to impact people outside of his corner of the world. Francis and the earliest brothers were already leaving the diocese to preach the gospel and invite people to join in greater imitation of Christ. Jurisdictional disputes over preaching had been cause for challenges to other lay groups equally as sincere and committed to their faith as Francis and his companions. In fact, given the many levels of controversy over authority, within church

formalized version of this time period, compare his account with that of Bonaventure (*Life of St. Francis*, 2:8).

44. "When blessed Francis saw that the Lord God was daily increasing their numbers, he wrote for himself and his brothers present and future, simply and in few words, a form of life and a rule. He used primarily words of the holy gospel, longing only for its perfection. He inserted a few other things necessary for the practice of a holy way of life. Then he went to Rome with all his brothers, since he greatly desired that the Lord Pope Innocent the Third confirm for him what he had written." Thomas of Celano, *Life of Saint Francis*, 1:13:32, in Armstrong et al., *The Saint*, 210. To compare Celano's version with other accounts, see *Anonymous of Perugia*, ch. 7, in Armstrong et al., *The Founder*, 48–51, and *The Legend of the Three Companions*, ch. 12, in Armstrong et al., *The Founder*, 95–99.

and society, it would have been irresponsible for Francis to have sent his companions out into foreign territory without some way of protecting them from situations that might lead to misunderstanding or accusations of heresy.

What is also important to understand is that many, many forms of religious life had been created throughout the twelfth century, nearly all of them responding to the ethical and spiritual crisis triggered by the rise of urban economies. Many saw the urgent need for an authentic witness of poverty and accompaniment; increasingly, this became a moral and spiritual imperative as Europe's feudal, agrarian economic system gave way to the complexities of a market-based economy and urban centers ate through the poor and left them, literally, to die on the streets. This spirituality had to prophetically demonstrate how to live gospel values in the face of a grinding poverty that could not be hidden in hovels at the corners of vast tracts of land. By Francis's time, the "apostolic life" as modeled by Jesus and the community of men and women who surrounded him had become one of the most credible forms of religious life. As Bernard McGinn notes:

> One of the most remarkable things about this new understanding of the *vita apostolica* in the twelfth and thirteenth centuries is how rapidly the evangelical ideal, which found its scriptural warrant in the picture of Christ sending out the disciples to preach without "purse, or wallet, or sandals" in Luke 10:1–12 and parallel passages, spread to all levels of society.[45]

There was both desire and demand for the authentic witness of apostolic poverty, simplicity, and preaching, spurring reform of religious life at all levels.

Of course, models of conversion to Christ epitomized by dramatic renunciation were already an integral part of the Christian tradition's understanding of what it was to be holy.[46] However, the call to "go

---

45. Bernard McGinn, *Flowering of Mysticism*, 6. For a study of the effects of this ideal on religious life see Lester K. Little, *Religious Poverty and the Profit Economy in Medieval Europe* (Ithaca, NY: Cornell University Press, 1978).

46. In fact, conversion as a direct response to hearing the gospel call "Go, sell all you have, give to the poor, and come follow me" dates all the way back to the late third century, when the prototypical saint, Antony, renounced his patrimony and gradually moved to Egypt, becoming at first a hermit

and sell all you have" to follow Christ in poverty took on renewed meaning and urgency in the twelfth and thirteenth centuries because the growing market-based economy challenged Christians to strip themselves of an identity forged by social status and economic standing and devote themselves more explicitly to simplicity and the social principles of the gospel. As Lester K. Little cogently argued several decades ago, medieval urbanization led to new concerns about the ethical responsibility of Christians toward the increasingly disenfranchised poor. In a rural society, serfs, for all that their lives might be miserable, were critical to the agricultural survival of the entire feudal system. Landowners could not let them starve. In an urban society, responsibility for the care of the lowest socioeconomic class was a great deal more ambiguous. Traditional forms of monasticism, themselves so heavily rooted in feudal society and in withdrawal from the world, were not able to engage the apostolic life, much less the care of the poor, which also overwhelmed traditional ecclesiastical forms of charity distributed by bishops. Ordinary Christians of all sorts stepped in to fill the gap, from the Humiliati in Lombardy and Milan to the Beguines to the Waldensians, followers of a cloth merchant of Lyons named Peter Valdes.[47] All of these groups were committed to modeling the ideals of the gospel in new forms of Christian communities. Just how distinguishable from them would Francis and his fledgling community have been? Papal approval and formal recognition of Francis and his way of life were critical in that they gave Francis and his companions the freedom to continue to explore the presence of Christ who was known in poverty and simple human fellowship.

What Francis wanted to recapture and live was what the earliest companions of Christ had experienced: the presence of God coming alive in the human community. He wanted that to be the universal Christian way. Francis saw the living God in the discarded, and he wanted everyone else to be able to see God, too. He understood the

and then the "father of monasticism." See Athanasius, *Life of Antony*, par. 2, in Athanasius, *The Life of Antony and the Letter to Marcellinus*, trans. Robert C. Gregg (New York: Paulist Press, 1980).
47. See Little, *Religious Poverty*, 113–45.

forces that he and his contemporaries were up against. He saw how his own neighbors closed their eyes to the suffering poor, built walls to protect their consciences, and even discarded those who were unproductive. But in leper colonies and at the margins, God was showing him how to remedy human exploitation through a tenderness that cherished those considered worthless. And the joy of seeing God come alive once again was not something he could keep to himself.

I am not certain that Francis was particularly interested in church structures, nor even, really, in the church as an institutional body. He was interested in establishing a home for God in the human community. He wanted everyone to pursue a shared desire and a shared commitment to find Christ incarnate in our midst, without walls and without exclusion, and he did not think that any endeavor short of that was particularly Christian. In human terms, he was interested in being what child psychiatrist Alice Miller called an "enlightened witness," someone who, through kindness, tenderness, and focused, intense love, can return people back to themselves.[48] Francis's sense of church was one of constant extension, solidarity, accompaniment, and communion. In fact, in many ways, Francis's embodiment of poverty, simplicity, and tender care was a way of teaching the church what it was to be a genuine community. For some, it was a reminder of gospel values forgotten after decades of civil and ecclesiastical conflict over wealth, territory, and power. For others, it was a new vision entirely. For all, however, there was a definitive stirring of the Spirit—a radical attentiveness to the demands of the gospel resulting in something that increasingly felt revolutionary.

As they walked back to Assisi, Francis and his companions contemplated their new status within the church at large, asking themselves how they could best be a living example of the gospel. They stopped near the city of Orte for about two weeks to allow their new way of life to crystallize for them, committing themselves to the daily precariousness of the poor and homeless by begging each day for the food they needed to sustain themselves.[49] When they continued

---

48. Cf. Boyle, *Tattoos on the Heart*, 192.

on their way, they spoke with greater confidence about the gospel message, "proclaiming the kingdom of God and preaching peace and penance for the remission of sins, not in the persuasive words of human wisdom but in the learning and power of the Holy Spirit." In describing Francis's new-found confidence, Celano writes that Francis

first convinced himself by action and then convinced others by words. Not fearing anyone's rebuke, he spoke the truth boldly, so that even well-educated men, distinguished by fame and dignity, were amazed at his words and shaken by a healthy fear in his presence.[50]

The personal charism and authenticity of Francis's witness, combined now with papal approval of his way of life, led to rapid and exponential expansion of Francis's experiment in community. The movement toward more authentic imitation of the gospel aroused both great hope and renewed commitment in Francis's contemporaries—women as well as men.

Clare, for one, was ready to become an active and equal partner with Francis in this gospel way of life. We have already noted her significant financial and moral support for the movement. But until this way of life had some kind of official status within the church, far beyond the support that the local bishop could offer, it would have been just about impossible for Clare to join forces more actively with him. I suspect, however, that Clare had already been mentally preparing to join the reform and was merely awaiting Francis's return from Rome with papal approval before cutting the final cord to her life within the city walls. Clare's childhood friend Bona of Guelfuccio testified that Clare had given her money to take down to "those who were working on Saint Mary of the Portiuncula so that they would sustain the flesh," thus

49. Thomas of Celano, *Life of Saint Francis*, 1:14:35, in Armstrong et al., *The Saint*, 214: "There, they began to have commerce with holy poverty. Greatly consoled in their lack of all things of the world, they resolved to adhere to the way they were in that place always and everywhere. Only divine consolation delighted them, having put aside all their cares about earthly things. They decided and resolved that even if buffeted by tribulations and driven by temptations they would not withdraw from its embrace."

50. Thomas of Celano, *Life of Saint Francis*, 1:15:36, in Armstrong et al., *The Saint*, 215. Thomas of Celano suggests that Francis's increased confidence was directly related to the papal approbation he had just received: "He acted confidently in all matters because of the apostolic authority granted him."

confirming Clare's active collaboration with Francis in this new way of life as early as 1208 or 1209, since the brothers completed the church before they went to Rome for papal approval.[51]

The testimony of the women who knew Clare best supports this emerging portrait of a woman of conviction, commitment, prudence, and courage, prepared to offer her spiritual giftedness to what she understood to be the most authentic version of the gospel life she could embrace. Lady Bona, who had accompanied Clare as a chaperone during her early conversations with Francis, was aware that the two of them together had developed a plan that would allow Clare to enter Francis's way of life.[52] Clare's biological sister Beatrice testified that Francis approached Clare, after having heard of her holiness, almost as if he went to recruit her.

> After Saint Francis heard of the fame of her holiness, he went many times to preach to her, so that the virgin Clare acquiesced to his preaching, renounced the world and all earthly things, and went to serve God as soon as she was able. After that she sold her entire inheritance and part of that of the witness and gave it to the poor.[53]

The fact that Beatrice says that Clare went "as soon as she was able," underscores the need for the institutional stability of Francis's way of life before women could leave their households to join him.

Clare's departure from the world inside the city walls was no less

---

51. "The Seventeenth Witness," in *Acts of the Process of Canonization*, 17:7, in Armstrong, *The Lady*, 193: "Lady Clare, while she was still in the world, also gave the witness a certain amount of money as a votive offering and directed her to carry it to those who were working on Saint Mary of the Portiuncula so that they would sustain the flesh."

52. Ibid., 192: "Lady Clare was always considered by everyone a most pure virgin and had such fervor of spirit she could serve God and please Him. Because of this, the witness many times accompanied her to speak to Saint Francis. She went secretly as not to be seen by her parents. Asked what Saint Francis said to her, she replied he always preached to her about converting to Jesus Christ. Brother Philip did the same. She listened willingly to him and consented to all the good things said to her." Bona's account would date these conversations to 1210–11, prior to Clare's being received by Francis into this new way of life "more than forty-two years" before Bona's testimony on November 28, 1253.

53. "The Twelfth Witness," in *Acts of the Process of Canonization*, 12:2–3, in Armstrong, *The Lady*, 183. Beatrice suggests that Clare's generosity may have exceeded her actual claims to her family's wealth. This would help contextualize her family's ire and their pursuit of her to the church of San Paolo de Abbadesse, which Beatrice proceeds to narrate directly after this, suggesting a causal link between "she sold her entire inheritance and part of that of the witness" and "her relatives wanted to drag her out [of the church]." See ibid., par. 4, and see discussion below.

dramatic than Francis's own. Late at night on Palm Sunday, Clare escaped from her family's palace, hurried down the narrow city streets, and passed through the gates of the city walls for the last time in her life. It is not difficult at all to imagine young Clare's excitement, after months of planning and preparation. Slipping out under cover of night, she successfully made her way through the valley to the Portiuncula where Francis and several companions waited for her. Once Francis had tonsured and clothed her in a habit and veil, they departed for the Benedictine convent of San Paolo delle Abbadesse about four kilometers from Assisi.

Of all the options Clare might have had for safe haven, Francis and Clare had chosen this destination because a papal bull of Innocent III dated May 5, 1201, granted the community broad and specific rights of asylum to take in women in distress. The edict forbade the use of violence against the women under the pain of excommunication. Clare had likely anticipated the active resistance of the men in her family to her decision to embrace poverty and the apostolic life, and had chosen a place where she could expect safety and insulation from any ill treatment from her family.

It was all the more shocking, then, that the very next day, Clare's male relatives pursued her and stormed into the monastery's chapel in order to bring her home by force if necessary.[54] In an attempt to escape their wrath and protect herself, Clare grabbed the altar cloths, claiming the right of the convent's sanctuary and special protections. Uncovering her head to show the men that they were too late, she revealed her shorn hair, the physical evidence that she had already vowed herself to God and made herself unmarriageable. Her younger sister recounts, "In no way did she acquiesce, neither letting them take her from that place nor remaining with them."[55] Thomas of Celano's *Life of Saint Clare* describes:

---

54. See Thomas of Celano, *The Life of Saint Clare*, 6: "But after the news reached her relatives, they condemned with a broken heart the deed and proposal of the virgin and, banding together as one, they ran to the place. . . . They employed violent force, poisonous advice, and flattering promises, persuading her to give up such a worthless deed that was unbecoming to her class and without precedent in her family."

55. "The Twelfth Witness," in *Acts of the Process of Canonization*, 12:4, in Armstrong, *The Lady*, 183.

> With the increasing violence of her relatives, her spirit grew and her love—provoked by injuries—provided strength. . . . Amid words and deeds of hatred, she molded her spirit anew in hope until her relatives, turning back, were quiet.[56]

Clare had won the first battle and now, without the need for asylum, she moved to the church of Sant' Angelo in Panzo, a small monastery of penitential women, which seemed more suited to the poverty she desired.[57] Clare had thwarted her family's grandiose plans to marry her off and protect their wealth for future generations, and the men in the family smoldered. They did not anticipate a mass exodus as many of Clare's female relatives joined her.

The first of these was Clare's sister Catherine, who appeared at the church of Sant' Angelo fifteen days after Clare had slipped away, confiding to her sister her own desire to join the new gospel way. This turn of events caught Francis and Clare by surprise, and they were less prepared for the next confrontation with the Offreduccio men, who became even more violent at the realization that they had lost another of the family's most treasured assets. Twelve knights appeared at the church of Sant' Angelo to bring Catherine home by force, for she had not yet been tonsured. The knights began to strike Catherine, ripping her clothes and crippling her with blows.

Reconstructing this scene from the sources, Joan Mueller writes:

> When the knights of the family heard that Catherine escaped, they went to the humble and unfortified Monastery of Sant'Angelo, captured Catherine, and when she resisted their efforts to take her back home, beat her until she seemed lifeless. Perhaps too embarrassed to bring back into town a young woman ignobly beaten by men whose honor depended on providing her protection, they rode off, leaving Agnes for dead.[58]

Clare nursed her back to life, and when Francis arrived to receive Catherine and tonsure her, he suggested that she take the name

---

56. Thomas of Celano, *Life of Saint Clare*, 9.
57. The best reconstruction of these events is contained in Mueller, *Privilege of Poverty*, 7–16.
58. Mueller, *Clare of Assisi*, 12–13. Compare this version with the account in Mueller, *Privilege of Poverty*, 10–12, which summarizes the hagiographical accounts.

"Agnes" after the early Christian martyr because of the violence she had suffered.[59]

I have recounted Clare's personal story at some length because this context helps us to understand that there was a deep strategy to the community that Francis and Clare were creating. Neither of them was a stranger to trauma and violence; their communities of solidarity and care were havens from outside forces, even as they were spaces of creative resistance and transformation. Further, their context is not all that different from our own. Clare's experience of violence in the home asks us to be aware of how deeply and intimately violence can permeate our personal lives, especially if we are women. We cannot afford to ignore the reality that the relationships that are supposed to provide support, comfort, solace, and joy are so often toxic and even lethal. Adrienne Rich once famously called the family home the most dangerous place in America for women, and the Centers for Disease Control and Prevention estimates that the annual costs of intimate partner violence against women exceed $5.8 billion.[60] We ignore the epidemic of violence against women at our own peril and cannot speak of human well-being without ensuring that homes and families are safe for women and children. As Pope Francis reminds us, our first and fundamental response to the gospel, the good news that gives life, is "to desire, seek and protect the good of others."[61] While guaranteeing protection from violence and discrimination is an important first step, there is also the work of "growing into a solidarity that would allow all peoples to become the artisans of their destiny, since 'every person is called to self-fulfillment.'"[62]

---

59. Other women from Clare's family who joined her at San Damiano included Clare's niece Balvina, daughter of Sir Martino of Coccorano, in about 1220; Clare's youngest sister, Beatrice, who entered San Damiano in 1229; and another of Clare's nieces, Amata, sister of Balvina. Clare's mother, Ortulana, joined Clare as well, but the date of her entrance is uncertain.

60. National Center for Injury Prevention and Control, *Costs of Intimate Partner Violence Against Women in the United States* (Atlanta: Centers for Disease Control and Prevention, 2003), http://tinyurl.com/jkop4f8. One in four women has been the victim of "severe physical violence" by her intimate partner in her lifetime, and the long-term health consequences to this violence (whether it is permanent disability, chronic health conditions, homelessness, or stress-induced physical or psychological symptoms) are devastating.

61. Pope Francis, *Joy of the Gospel*, par. 178.

62. Ibid., par. 190.

As we begin to explore Francis and Clare's gospel way, it is helpful to remember that we need to ground the practice of tenderness in the world in which we live: a world that is often hostile, toxic, and even lethal to some of its most tender members. This way of tenderness requires an inner resolve, a steely strength, and a tenacity that might at first seem to contradict what we stereotypically think of as "tenderness." Over and over, as we contemplate the example of their lives, Francis and Clare will surprise us. They were strategic, successfully predicting the violent response of Clare's male relatives and doing everything they could to counter its impact; they were profoundly courageous, taking risks in order to ensure that their movement grew and thwarting resistance on many fronts; and they understood the need to create a protective space for the nurturance of the relationships that give life. They understood, in short, and committed themselves to "a new and universal solidarity"[63] that had the capacity to change the predominant paradigm of their day.

Francis and Clare's prophetic stance in rejecting all dehumanizing elements of life models what Pope Francis in The Joy of the Gospel has called "evangelical discernment." Francis and Clare give us a clear criterion for how to engage such discernment. They rejected whatever diminished or devalued the holiness of each human encounter, and therefore they model for us how to say "no" to the many forces in our world that "threaten the life and dignity of God's people."[64] As the drama of their initial conversion gives way to the larger context of forming life-giving communities of care, hope, and vision, they help us see how our deepening conversion to solidarity creates a space for God to come alive more fully in our own world. For Francis and Clare, radical poverty (saying "no" to all that dehumanizes us) is concurrently a way to make more space for the indwelling presence of God in our communities. Pope Francis's appeal to us to understand, accept, and embrace "our mutual belonging" is a powerful way of

---

63. Pope Francis, *Laudato Si'*, par. 14.
64. Pope Francis, *Joy of the Gospel*, par. 51.

expressing this kind of conversion, so necessary for our world today. He writes:

> Many things have to change course, but it is we human beings above all who need to change. We lack an awareness of our common origin, of our mutual belonging, and of a future to be shared with everyone. This basic awareness would enable the development of new convictions, attitudes and forms of life. A great cultural, spiritual and educational challenge stands before us, and it will demand that we set out on the long path of renewal."[65]

As dramatic and important as Francis and Clare's initial acts of renunciation were, their choices were merely the first of a long series of "choices toward" the deepening of their dedication to the gospel life and the love that God grows within us as we choose toward that way of life. For those of us who choose to walk in the footsteps of Francis and Clare, choice becomes a question of how we make use of all of our thoughtful, deliberative, and affective capacities. Choice becomes a growing capacity to discern the implications and consequences of our choices, a growing capacity to weigh and assess what will best lead to the deepening of God's life within us and within our world, a growing commitment to prioritizing actions and approaches that protect and safeguard our inner simplicity, our reverence for creation, self and other.

In short, choice becomes a deliberate, intentional, and life-long decision to be faithful to the process of collaborating with the unfolding mystery of God in our lives. When we truly dedicate ourselves to God, we find, as Francis and Clare did, that we are dedicating ourselves to an evolving partnership that has no end and no limits, a partnership whose end we cannot entirely know or predict. For such a process to be set fully in motion requires a set of commitments, supports, and even freedoms from social expectations and cultural norms that may look to us, initially, as only privations.

---

65. Pope Francis, *Laudato Si'*, par. 202.

On pilgrimage, when we trace these dramatic moments, we pause, at the end of "Conversion Day," to reflect on how radical but life-giving Francis and Clare's "yes" to God really was. Saying "no" to so much allowed them to experience a deeper fullness, of God and of life, than they could have known within the confines of the city walls or the lives that their culture and society required of them. Perhaps what should stand out for us, as we consider their example, was their early clarity that to embrace a life of joy and meaning and authenticity required them to literally opt out of the economic, social, political, and even religious dimensions of a world that encroached upon and threatened their very souls. In doing so, they said "no," directly and indirectly, to the people that were closest to them—family members and friends who could not help but take personally their rejection. But the poverty that Francis and Clare chose was "not a kind of penurious poverty that demands hardship without love." In fact, it was a poverty embraced in order to love more fully and completely,[66] a poverty that allowed Francis and Clare to learn how to dwell in the graciousness of God.[67]

Francis and Clare said "no" to their families with their myriad of expectations and gave up their socioeconomic status in order to embrace a way of life. But perhaps we forget that this was a way of life that had to be created as they went. It wasn't as if they walked out of one world and right into another. Francis puts this simply, even starkly, in his *Testament*, at the end of his life, when he writes: "No one showed me what I had to do." Only slowly and gradually did "the Most High reveal to me that I should live according to the pattern of the Holy Gospel."[68] Francis and Clare had to discover, uncover, and

---

66. Mueller, *Privilege of Poverty*, 20. Thus Mueller declares: "Franciscans do not choose poverty because they are seeking the contempt of the world, but because they are willing to suffer the contempt of the world in order to be with the person that they truly love." Later she writes that Francis and Clare's poverty "is a response of giving all for the sake of the one that one loves. It is a relational faith that God will take care of one if one takes care of the business of God" (Ibid., 24).

67. "Graciousness dignifies human presence and when it is present, it brings out the best in people. It opens a perspective which enables us to *see* the gifts that we have. It creates an atmosphere which awakens nobility of mind and heart. A gracious mind has compassion and sensitive understanding. It is without greed; rather than concentrating on what is absent or missing, it is able to celebrate and give thanks for what is present." John O'Donohue, *Beauty: The Invisible Embrace* (New York: HarperCollins, 2004), 52–53.

68. Francis of Assisi, *Testament*, 14, in Armstrong et al., *The Saint*, 125.

create together an environment and a community that was conducive to honoring God at all times and in all places—in the poor and despised, in the meek and suffering. It was in the small, the simple, the unnoticed, and the overlooked spaces that they were able to find and behold the God they sought: a God of gentleness and grace who constantly showed mercy and tender care.

I think that each of them, in their own way, came to the conclusion that it was far easier to find that God by letting go of everything—all expectations, all demands on time, all considerations, and, certainly, all concerns and anxieties over possessions and upkeep of property—and, instead, celebrating the miracle of there always being enough, between the kindness of friends and strangers and the generosity of God, to move us to be thankful rather than resentful. If this is a new way of being human, it is a way both of gratitude and human resourcefulness—a movement to notice, honor, and take delight in the human capacity to be generous, kind, and attentive to one another.

It is also important to note that Francis and Clare chose joy. We so often see their renunciation as a kind of noble sacrifice, but I am not at all sure that they experienced their choices in that way. Their embrace of spiritual joy through simplicity and the celebration of the presence of God in daily life is an often overlooked but essential element of the Franciscan way. One cannot visit Assisi and fail to experience their radiant joy, which permeates the city even today. While it is easy to focus on their embrace of poverty, Francis and Clare knew that, in some ways, their wealthy contemporaries, enmeshed in the defense of their wealth and any number of generational feuds, were far more impoverished than they. In their early years, Francis and Clare saw the poverty of anger, bitterness, and revenge and chose, instead, loving kindness, joy, and the fullness of life that generosity invites.[69]

In a world as confused about pleasure as ours is, it is probably also

---

69. Francis "mandated" the practice of joy, cheer, and graciousness in his rule of 1221, writing: "Wherever the brothers may be and in whatever place they meet, they should respect spiritually and attentively one another, and honor one another without complaining. Let them be careful not to appear outwardly as sad and gloomy hypocrites but show themselves joyful, cheerful and consistently gracious in the Lord." See Francis of Assisi, *The Earlier Rule*, 7:15, in Armstrong et al., *The Saint*, 69.

important not to assume too early that we know what true joy is. What so often passes for delight and pleasure can easily pull us from the purity of heart that fills us with vitality and helps us to see ourselves and the world around us in ways that are constantly fresh. The joy that I speak of here is a joy rooted in simplicity of spirit. Our hearts may know and sense it, but we might settle, out of habit, for something far less than the kind of joy we can discover in and with God, in and with one another. This is a joy like that of finding something that we thought was lost, a joy that scripture likens to that of finding a lost sheep, a lost coin, or, more to the point, the joy of recovering a loved one, as in the case of the return of the prodigal son.[70] It is a joy rooted in the realization of our deepest hopes and dreams. It is a joy that one cannot realize on one's own, for it is a joy that, by its intrinsic nature, seeks to be shared. It is a joy born of love, and, because it is rooted in a relational reality that endures, it is also a joy that is not predicated on particular outcomes or demands. As Pope Francis notes, "Joy adapts and changes, but it always endures, even as a flicker of light born of our personal certainty that, when everything is said and done, we are infinitely loved."[71] The joy that Francis and Clare knew and, in turn, shared with others, was the joy of life-giving love.

Choosing joy is not always possible in a world of suffering, particularly when our suffering is enmeshed in cycles of violence. Violence is traumatizing, and it is right that we not only seek "deliverance from evil" but also that we protect others from it. Both Francis and Clare personally experienced violence—Francis both in the battlefield and at the hands of his father, Clare at the hands of her own male relatives. Both were able to see clearly that such a response was inappropriate and even sinful. They neither condoned nor, more importantly, acquiesced to such behavior. Instead, they turned their backs, definitively, on the relationships that compromised their growing sense of purpose, dignity, and integrity as friends of God, choosing, instead, the joy of an entirely new way of life. They sought

70. See Luke 15.
71. Pope Francis, *Joy of the Gospel*, par. 6.

and created safe space, in other words, for their relationship with God to grow, realizing that putting oneself in circumstances that support one's inner integrity and capacity to love wholeheartedly is a deeply important choice toward God. It is an integral part of the movement toward the deepening of God's life in us and in our world.

Thus we should notice attentively, as we try to apply their insights into our circumstances today, that Francis and Clare did not establish this new way of life in their own homes or on top of structures that were, in their experience, functionally unsound and incoherent when viewed in light of the values embodied by Christ. Cognizant of the toxicities of their culture, they chose not to adapt the gospel to the norms of their day but rather to create new norms that called all people to see one another differently. They taught accountability, embracing the freedom of poverty and marginality as a foundation for the creation of an entirely new human family.

Francis and Clare understood the corrosive effects of an unloving environment—all that might fall under today's categories of "dysfunction" and "abuse"—and they separated themselves from contact with all that might compromise their integrity, reengaging the world from a space of inner stability and within a community that supported the fruition of their search for deeper relationship with God. Dwelling in the sacred space of relationship with God was critical so that they could engage the world lovingly. Perhaps part of their great wisdom is that, while they sensed that they were capable of great love, they did not expect themselves to love in the wholehearted way they desired without the support of a similarly dedicated, intentionally formed community. From what we now know about trauma— especially that of deeply patterned abuse, such as repeated experiences of childhood abuse—there is much wisdom here in recognizing and honoring the fragility of the human spirit and embracing our genuine need for community support in order to thrive as loving persons. For some of us—many of us, if we consider the statistics—this will require extricating ourselves from situations and relationships that wound our spirits and threaten our well-being in order to seek and create the relationships that love us into greater life.

The Franciscan legacy is not naïve. For all of their aspirations to simplicity, Francis and Clare also recognized that they had to be "wise as serpents" even as they were "gentle as doves."[72] Their choice toward God was practical and replete with understanding of the human condition. They recognized the toxicity of their world, and they sought to create an alternative space in which the love of God could flourish. The way of gentleness they embraced—the dwelling place for God they prepared in their hearts and in the communities they grew—had no room for anger or bitterness, but that certainly did not mean that they excused, justified, or tolerated violence and indignity. Instead, they sought, uncompromisingly, to create a space where purity of heart could flourish, where a serenity rooted in the wisdom of the Spirit could grow. This was possible only in a space of deepest safety, learning anew the gift of love and the gift of life in relationship with the One who is supremely trustworthy. Francis and Clare model for us the often necessary separation from toxic environments that frees us first to create new communities of possibility and second to work with new strength and support to transform the world. This paradigm becomes a more viable strategy for meaningful change than working within a system that is unable or unwilling to be self-critical or to set aside its lethal ways. As Albert Einstein reputedly observed: "No problem can be solved by the same level of consciousness that created it." If it is true that imagination is more important than knowledge, it is the collaborative will to imagine a different way that we lack.

Solving our problems requires us to grow beyond the smallnesses of character and vision that plague us, uncovering together a solidarity that dignifies and creates possibilities that, individually, we are unable to create. If love is, in the end, "the *only* light which 'can always illuminate a world grown dim and give us the courage needed to keep

---

72. Matthew 10:16. In fact, Francis cites this verse directly in his *Earlier Rule (Regula non bullata)* in his comments about how the brothers are to comport themselves when they "go among the Saracens and Other Non Believers." See *Earlier Rule* 16:2, in Armstrong et al., *The Saint*, 74: "Therefore, be prudent as serpents and simple as doves."

living and working,'"[73] we shall need to allow and enable love to give us the new human intelligence that our species currently requires. For love is not just a transforming power. It is the only viable strategy we have left.

73. Pope Francis, *Joy of the Gospel*, par. 272.

4

———

The Revolution of Tenderness: Practicing *Misericordia* and *Communio*

Image 4a. Francis's Encounter with the Leper. Mural at the Sanctuary of La Verna.

Everyone needs to be touched by the comfort and attraction of God's saving love, which is mysteriously at work in each person, above and beyond their faults and failings.[1]

Francis and Clare had achieved, through their tenacity and active renunciation, the freedom to create a whole new way of life. From early on, they knew that this "new way" was a complete immersion into the gospel life, to live as Jesus and his companions had. But there was still so much to learn about how to live such a life, how to sustain it in community, and how to nurture a dedicated and life-giving communal relationship with God that would provide inner light and direction for daily life. If we are to understand what was truly revolutionary about Francis and Clare's way of embodying the gospel life, we must identify the core spiritual values that they modeled.

In the previous chapter, we explored how encounter with God at the margins of existence led Francis and Clare to transforming relationships developed in an ever-expanding community of mutual investment and concern. We described the conversion and dedication that such relationships require. We have already suggested that tenderness is an intrinsic part of the transformative process that moves us beyond "encounter" and toward communion. Tenderness is one way to approach the dynamic of *misericordia* that Francis describes in his *Testament*; grasping that dynamic, so that we might know its transforming power, is the task of this chapter.

Tenderness is a learned habit, an acquired sensitivity born of solidarity and keen interest in the lives, challenges, struggles, and joys of others. We do not become tender because we want to, just like we do not become fit because we want to. Desire is important, but dedication is even more critical. We dedicate ourselves to growth in tenderness, just as we might to greater fitness or flexibility.

While it is common to read about the early Franciscan focus on poverty and preaching and even their imitation of Christ, these phrases fail to convey what was special, even revolutionary, about

---

1. Pope Francis, *Joy of the Gospel*, par. 44.

their way of life. Their evangelization, or sharing of the gospel,[2] was intended to be a direct communication of the life-giving love of God. It responded directly to the question: "For if we have received the love which restores meaning to our lives, how can we fail to share that love with others?"[3] Deeper and more direct than preaching with words, Francis and Clare directly communicated God's tender care and allowed people to see love in concrete, practical action: encouraging, supporting, sustaining, protecting, cherishing, admonishing. People acknowledged and joined the "Franciscan revolution" because Francis and Clare illuminated the truth of love's power. They made real the life-giving presence of God in the human community. As others saw the possibility of life-giving love, they, too, wanted to experience and contribute to its transformative impact on the world around them.

Francis and Clare made it easier to see and imitate God's love in practical actions that made a difference in people's lives. As Pedro Arrupe's poem suggests, falling in love and staying in love with the God who walks with us in the world does truly "change everything." And so we should be clear that our very identity is at stake as we walk together on this way of tenderness. Learning God's love is a profound corrective to much that we have learned from other sources. We will have to let go of many cherished ideas in order to learn things anew, particularly in the arena of love, since much of what our cultures and societies have taught us about love and desire is actively deceptive. Francis and Clare refine for us the challenge of being human, even as they helpfully illuminate the work of the Christian person: our challenge is to embrace an evolving identity deeply informed by the ways that God reveals Godself to us, with and through the needs of others.

---

2. Literally, spreading of the good news of Christ. Franciscans prefer to self-identify their way of life as "evangelical" rather than "apostolic," a claim they say that Francis never made himself. As long as the adjective "evangelical" is seen in the larger context of the many forms of apostolic life that were part of this twelfth and thirteenth century milieu, rather than as completely *sui generis*, this adjective can be helpful, because it conveys both the apostolic ideals of the early thirteenth century and the increased awareness of Jesus known through gospel story. I have chosen to use the phrase "gospel way of life" in what follows in favor of "apostolic life" or "evangelical life" to point toward a growing synthesis of both orientations—that is, to the *vita apostolica* as a religious ideal and to the example and witness of Christ known through the gospels.

3. Pope Francis, *Joy of the Gospel*, par. 8.

A phrase that has come to mean a great deal to me is probably appropriate here: "the pedagogy of God." When a friend first used this phrase with me, in the context of our conversation both about Ignatius Loyola's *Spiritual Exercises* and my friend's work with the poor in Peru who, he had already told me, were his most critical teachers, the phrase rang true and seemed pathfinding. ("I went to the University of Chicago," he said. "But the poor were my real teachers.") Simply and thoroughly, embracing the pedagogy of God at the margins challenges us to allow the incarnate God to be our primary teacher. And several questions proceed naturally from our response: How will we engage an intimate enough relationship with God to be taught at Christ's side, just as those closest to Jesus were? And what does the poverty of Christ, Christ's solidarity with the marginalized, and what the poor and disenfranchised have to teach us have to do with the way that God teaches and what God wants us to know? These, I would argue, were exactly the questions that drew Francis and Clare forward on the way of *misericordia*. They are, at heart, relational questions; they involve a commitment to a new form of identity, one predicated upon relationship. They lead to what Pope Francis has called "*la mística de vivir juntos*"—the mystical life that we share together. It is almost impossible to translate this profound and illuminating phrase into contemporary English because we have made the mystical life a phenomenon, not a reality in which we can and should live as a human family. But this is the invitation we face, underneath the chaos and challenge of our world: How will we embrace and support our living together in ways that honor God and dignify one another? Can this life truly be a sacred pilgrimage of encounters that enrich rather than transactions that degrade?[4]

Only if we are willing to grow, to be changed, to have our assumptions and presumptions challenged, especially as we heed the

---

4. Cf. Pope Francis, *Joy of the Gospel*, par. 87: "Today, when the networks and means of human communication have made unprecedented advances, we sense the challenge of finding and sharing a 'mystique' of living together, of mingling and encounter, of embracing and supporting one another, of stepping into this flood tide which, while chaotic, can become a genuine experience of fraternity, a caravan of solidarity, a sacred pilgrimage."

invitation to accompany the poorest and most marginalized, and courageously to denounce and change the systems that marginalize and degrade. This is a solidarity that changes lives, a "stay with me"[5] love that refuses to turn its back on the spaces of human darkness that many would rather ignore or deny: the trafficking of children, the degradation of women, slavery. All of the places where "hardness of heart" turns truly lethal and ugly, where human pathologies have led to suffering, depravity, and a sick intransigence that dishonors our dignity as a human community and as a species.

A genuine turn toward a transforming solidarity at the margins requires a new, relational identity (as opposed to a more autonomous one, predicated on our assumptions, our personal goals, and the priorities and values we inherit from our cultures). For many of us, this invitation is likely to be at least as disconcerting as Francis and Clare's insistence on material poverty. But if it is true that we need others to pull us out of the "smallness" of ourselves, then this relational identity is the cornerstone of a fertile creativity that grows as we join forces with others and allow the wellspring of the Spirit to release grace into the world through our connectedness.[6] This is a solidarity that gives life to all—not just the marginalized but us, too. What is ironic is that we continue to see Francis's and Clare's journeys in terms of renunciation—what they gave up—rather than in terms of what they gained: a genuine richness in the quality of their lives, as love and kinship grew and spread and they showed the world that there is no "them" and "us," just us.[7]

In this chapter, we turn to the heart of tenderness, to understand what constitutes "the tenderness of God," which I would correlate with the more technical term "*misericordia.*" I am going to use these two

---

5. Jesus's plea to his closest friends in the Garden of Gethsemane as he faced the most difficult hours of his life. See Mark 13:34, Matt 26:38.
6. See my comments on this relational identity as it relates to the insights of Teresa of Avila and John of the Cross in both Gillian T. W. Ahlgren, *Entering Teresa of Avila's* Interior Castle: A *Reader's Companion* (Mahwah, NJ: Paulist Press, 2005), 63–75, 102–9, and 113–20, and in Gillian T. W. Ahlgren, *Enkindling Love: The Legacy of Teresa of Avila and John of the Cross* (Minneapolis: Fortress Press, 2016), 11–15, 42–44, 52–53, and 115–20.
7. This strong sense of kinship is a prevalent theme in Greg Boyle's *Tattoos on the Heart*; see, for example, p. 190.

terms interchangeably, but it is important to attach and ground the more generic term "tenderness" with the word that Francis himself used to describe "the way that God had with me." Francis and Clare's experience, practice, and embodiment of this *misericordia* is what made their imitation of Christ authentic and illuminating to others. *Misericordia* is the spiritual and theological heart of their way of life, the heart of what they learned from God as they made the margins of society their home. I am also compelled by the deep need for us to understand what *misericordia* is (and what it is not) in light of the fact that Pope Francis invited the whole human race to consider this way of life when he declared a year of *misericordia* beginning on December 8, 2015.

It should be apparent, but I will state it clearly: the translation of *"misericordia"* in English as "mercy" is both inaccurate and unfortunate. To think of what Francis and Clare (or Jesus, for that matter) were about as "mercy" instead of a form of radical, committed, relational love that changes everything runs the risk of being actively misleading. *Misericordia* is a rich biblical, spiritual, and theological concept that moves far beyond the concept and practice of "mercy" and probes deeply whether or not the economic, social, and cultural structures in which we live are just and godly. Further, it asks us to live out our deepest ideals about goodness and right action in the context of all of our interpersonal encounters. "Mercy" is a poor equivalent for it can carry with it ideologies that we may not recognize, much less challenge and change. For some, "mercy" suggests little more than that those with money should be generous to those without or that those in power should be "merciful" to those who lack power. *Misericordia* as the practice of tenderness and *communio* exposes the assumptions of unequal power distribution and challenges the human community to live with the well-being of all constantly in mind.[8] In a world (past or

---

8. Cf. Pope Francis, *Joy of the Gospel*, par. 92: "The way to relate to others which truly heals instead of debilitating us, is a *mystical* fraternity, a contemplative fraternity. It is a fraternal love capable of seeing the sacred grandeur of our neighbor, of finding God in every human being, of tolerating the nuisances of life in common by clinging to the love of God, of opening the heart to divine love and seeking the happiness of others."

present) where impunity is often the rule, we need more clarity than ever about what *misericordia* is and what it is not.

My concern is far more than one of semantics. It is the concern of a theologian and human being who wants to be sure that we are actually listening to God and reading correctly the signs of our own times. We will not be able to hear what God wants to be teaching us about our intrinsic relatedness as sisters and brothers if we continue to think of *misericordia* as "mercy." What is "mercy" to the veteran who has lost everything—friends, faith in life, faith in authority, trust in the goodness of humanity, and her or his very soul? What is "mercy" to the woman who has repeatedly thrown her own body between her partner and her children, taking in violence that has no place whatsoever in our homes and families? What is mercy for the child who cries out for it every day, even as she is subjected to routine rape while others profit from her misery? The connotations of the word "mercy" may not help us move toward a culture of accountability and the praxis of a love that does justice, gives life, generates creativity, upholds dignity, and will not allow violence or abuse to trespass under the guise of family, community, or culture.

Rather than trying to redeem the word "mercy," it seems far better for us, whoever we are, to ask ourselves and one another what love truly is and to seek direct instruction from God about how tenderness can affirm dignity and enhance the life of God in the human community. This, I believe, is the conversation around *misericordia* that we all need and many of us want. It is certainly the conversation that will lead us to turn away from the kinds of defensiveness that keep us from the depths of our own humanity and instead learn how to embrace and support one another, to discover the intrinsic mystery of our relatedness as human beings created in and for love. This is the invitation to the gospel, which "tells us constantly to run the risk of face-to-face encounter with others, with their physical presence which challenges us, with their pain and their pleas, with their joy which infects us in our close and continuous interaction."[9] For *misericordia* is

9. Pope Francis, *Joy of the Gospel*, par. 88.

the very heart of the revolution of tenderness. It is the tender love that does justice, and it is, as the prophet Micah proclaims, the only thing that God asks of us: to act justly, love tenderly, and walk humbly with our God.[10] And it was *misericordia*, or loving kindness, that empowered Francis to reach out lovingly to others in the leper colony, to receive and be received in their community, and to find his way back to God and to his own humanity.[11] We have seen this line in his *Testament* already: "But then God Godself led me among them and I showed loving kindness [*feci misericordiam*] to them."[12] Francis's first direct experience of God was this moment when God "led him" amongst lepers. But what happened next, in terms of Francis's life, is easily obscured when we translate the phrase *"feci misericordiam"* as "I showed mercy."[13]

Scriptural Roots of *Misericordia*

Misericordia is a rich word in the world of scripture and Christian spirituality, reflecting a way that chooses love, compassion,

10. Micah 6:8.
11. As I sketch out what the "way of *misericordia*" looks like, as Francis and Clare embodied it, I shall attempt to correlate their lived theological insights with a larger tradition of Christian spirituality and with the specific challenges of the Christian church in the historical moment of the early thirteenth century, so that we can see how they bring the Christian tradition credibly into a new era of socioeconomic challenge. While *misericordia* as I define it here has not yet been identified as the "core" of the Franciscan way of life in previous studies, there is, of course, a great deal of consistency with earlier analyses, and it is my hope that this way of "naming" the Franciscan way of life will actually allow us to see greater depth, relevance, and meaning in traditional categories like "evangelization," "poverty," "imitation of Christ," "compassion," and "solidarity." Because *misericordia* is, fundamentally, an expression of divine generosity in a constant outpouring of love, its relationship to Trinitarian theology should always be highlighted. All that I describe in this chapter, then, should also be seen in the context of recent scholarly work arguing that Franciscan spirituality is a relational way of being, grounded in Trinitarian theology.
12. Francis of Assisi, *Testament*, 2, in Armstrong et al., *The Saint*, 124.
13. Regis Armstrong, J. A. Wayne Hellmann, and William J. Short, editors of the major English-language, three-volume collection of sources on Francis, indicate the significance of the phrase *"feci misericordiam"* which I am highlighting here, observing, rightly, that "The phrase *feci misericordiam* [I showed mercy] has a rich biblical tradition." They also correctly note that the phrase *facere misericordiam* appears almost fifty times in the Vulgate Bible, but then they fasten on a single, narrow aspect of the word: "Of these [biblical uses of the phrase *facere misericordiam*] the editors have chosen to suggest a reference to Sirach 35:4 "*qui faciet misericordiam offert sacrificum* [whoever shows mercy offers sacrifice]." Their translation of "*misericordia*" over the course of the three volumes is not always consistent. See their comments in Armstrong et al., *The Saint*, 124 n. c., and compare with their observation that *misericordia* is also a "heart sensitive to suffering." In Armstrong et al., *The Founder*, 534 n. b. This note would be much more helpful if it were contained in the note associated with the earlier text of Francis's *Testament* since Bonaventure actually uses the word "compassion" instead of the word "*misericordia*" to describe Francis's interactions with lepers.

commiseration, gentleness, kindness, and care rather than judgment, harshness, condemnation, or alienation. Over and over, both in the Jewish and Christian traditions, *misericordia* is developed as God's way of being in relation with us. A review of the Latin Vulgate Bible, which provided the basis for medieval written and oral scriptural tradition, shows the development of the concept of *misericordia* most pivotally in the Psalms, with important uses in the prophetic tradition of the Old Testament and in key gospel stories in the New Testament. In Isaiah, *misericordia* describes the restoration of relationship, the "great tenderness" and "enduring love" that God promises to Zion.[14] In the Psalms, *misericordia* is celebrated, again, as God's "enduring love," as in the repetition of Psalm 118, "Give thanks to the Lord, who is good, whose love [*misericordia*] endures forever."[15] This love is a love that "comforts,"[16] it is a "life-giving kindness"[17] that "safeguards" and protects us.[18] Thus, *misericordia* represents a relational reality of care that sustains human life: empowering, nurturing, challenging, comforting, protecting, and inspiring us.

Misericordia, like the love on which it is based, is not a single emotion, nor even merely a complex of emotions, nor a set of ways of interacting with another (e.g., mercifully). It expresses a way of being conditioned by our relationships with others, so that our concerns, orientations, and awareness are determined not only by what we see or feel or experience but also by the reality of others. *Misericordia* reflects an intersubjective reality, not entirely unlike being an expectant or nursing mother, where the movement or cries of another evoke a relational response from us. Phyllis Trible notes the maternal connotations of *misericordia*, explaining that the Hebrew word from

---

14. See especially Isa 54:7–10, in which the word *misericordia* is used twice along with other words to describe the quality of the feeling, culminating in 54:10 (New American Bible): "Though the mountains leave their place and the hills be shaken, My love [*misericordia*] shall never leave you."

15. Psalm 118:1, this use of *misericordia* is repeated in verses 2, 3, and 4 and used to end the psalm (v. 29). This repetition of "God's love endures forever" also occurs in Psalm 136.

16. Psalm 119:76: "May your love [*misericordia*] comfort me in accord with your promise to your servant."

17. Psalm 119:159: "In your kindness [*misericordia*] give me life."

18. Psalm 144:2. For a more extensive discussion of the concept of *misericordia* in scripture, see Walter Kasper, *Mercy: The Essence of the Gospel and the Key to Christian Life*, trans. William Madges (Mahwah, NJ: Paulist Press, 2014), 41–82.

which it is derived means, literally, "trembling womb."[19] The care and concern conveyed by the word is multifaceted, not immune to indignation and righteous anger, but constantly responsive to whatever is relationally appropriate for the well-being of the other. *Misericordia*, in other words, is an attentive, tender love that communicates direct and trustworthy presence. It is a deeply invested, active love that is protective, corrective, supportive, affirming, challenging, and whatever else the other needs for her or his deepest well-being.

That *misericordia* is a visceral love that spontaneously expresses commitment, concern, and active, constant involvement is what is at the heart of Pope Francis's decision to declare a year of *misericordia*. And that we have translated this *misericordia* in English as "mercy" is nothing short of tragic, particularly when the bull *Misericordia vultus* states clearly that God's *misericordia* is "not an abstract idea, but a concrete reality" that reveals the love "of a father or a mother, moved to the very depths out of love for their child."

> It is hardly an exaggeration to say that this is a "visceral" love. It gushes forth from the depths naturally, full of tenderness and compassion, indulgence and mercy.[20]

The spontaneity, immediacy, constancy, and trustworthiness of this love is what is critical. This is a love that never leaves us. It is also a love that surpasses our expectation—always surprising and even humbling us with its generosity. What an incredibly critical corrective for us today, in light of what so often passes for "love."

*   *   *

In the New Testament, Jesus models the *misericordia* of God over and over by being present to people in their suffering and sorrow and, whenever possible, relieving their burdens by and with his healing

---

19. Phyllis Trible, *God and the Rhetoric of Sexuality* (Philadelphia: Fortress Press, 1978), 31–59.
20. Pope Francis, *Misericordiae vultus* (Apostolic Letter, Rome, April 11, 2015) par. 6, http://tinyurl.com/je3fkdn.

presence. *"Misericordia"* is the motivation of the parent who, seeing a homecoming child from a distance, hurries to embrace him,[21] and it is the motivation of the good Samaritan, who came upon the injured man and was "moved with compassion at the sight."[22] When the gospels describe Jesus as being "moved with pity or compassion," they are pointing toward the *misericordia* that Jesus both felt and communicated to others, adding a richly expressive dimension to the human-divine relationship.[23]

Further, *misericordia* becomes the most appropriate antonym and antidote to Jesus's greatest complaint against his contemporaries: hardness of heart. *Misericordia* reflects a heart that is rich, generous, and expressive. It is that heart's fullness of tenderness and compassion, rather than the single quality of what is contained in the heart, that is more apropos, since the rich suppleness of a full heart gives us a broad range of creative responses to offer in love. Francis seems to capture this in his *Admonitions* when he writes:

Where there is a *misericordia* and discernment,
There is neither excess nor hardness of heart.[24]

In his analysis of the biblical connotations of the word "compassion," as Jesus embodies it, Albert Nolan argues that "compassion" is "far too weak" a concept to express this *misericordia*, or the impulse of

---

21. Luke 15:20 (NAB): "While he was still a long way off, his father caught sight of him, and was filled with compassion. He ran to his son, embraced him and kissed him."
22. Luke 10:33.
23. A brief but helpful summary of examples of Jesus's compassion is contained in Albert Nolan's discussion of Jesus's relationship with the poor: "'He was 'moved with compassion for the crowds and he healed their sick' (Matt 14:14). 'He was moved with compassion because they were distressed and dejected like sheep without a shepherd' (Matt 9:36, compare Mark 6:34). He was moved with compassion by the plight and the tears of the widow of Nain. 'Do not cry,' he says to her (Luke 7:13). We are told explicitly that he had compassion on a leper (Mark 1:41), on two blind men (Matt 20:34) and on those who had nothing to eat (Mark 8:2 par). Throughout the gospels, even when the word is not used, we can feel the movement of compassion. Over and over again Jesus says to people, 'Don't cry,' 'Don't worry,' 'Don't be afraid' (e.g., Mark 5:36, 6:50, Matt 6:25-34; see also Mark 4:40, Luke 10:41)." Albert Nolan, *Jesus before Christianity* (Maryknoll, NY: Orbis: 2003), 34–35.
24. See *Admonitions* 27:6 in Armstrong et al., *The Saint*, 137, which has, "Where there is a heart full of mercy and discernment, there is neither excess nor hardness of heart," along with the explanatory note: "The translator has again taken the liberty of translating *misericordia* more freely as 'a heart full of mercy.' This translation follows the more etymological sense of the word, *miser cor*, that is, a heart sensitive to misery."

Jesus toward others. English, he says, does not really have a word to describe this deep and visceral movement from "the intestines, bowels, entrails or heart"—that is, "the inward parts from which strong emotions seem to arise . . . a movement or impulse that wells up from one's very entrails . . . an eminently human feeling."[25] For Jesus, this feeling of compassion often extended itself into acts of healing and the restoration of the inherent dignity of the marginalized human person, often in practices as simple and concrete as conversation and meal sharing. As Nolan notes,

> It would be impossible to overestimate the impact these meals must have had upon the poor and the sinners. By accepting them as friends and equals Jesus had taken away their shame, humiliation and guilt. By showing them that they mattered to him as people he gave them a sense of dignity. . . . The physical contact which he must have had with them when reclining at table . . . must have made them feel clean and acceptable.[26]

Seen in this light, compassion goes beyond a movement to be of assistance to the other, because it "ineluctably entails a movement of participation in the experience of the other in order to be present and available in solidarity and communion. Compassion requires sensitivity to what is weak and/or wounded, as well as the vulnerability to be affected by the other. It also demands action to alleviate pain and suffering."[27] In Nolan's analysis of Jesus's interactions, Jesus's simple but sincere gestures of friendship and acceptance resulted in "a kind of healing or salvation," which was experienced as "relief, joy, gratitude and love."[28] Such insights into the community Jesus gathered around him help us appreciate Francis's orientation to the leper colonies, both as foundational to his own spiritual growth and as a source of formation for newcomers to the gospel way, the way of God's love. It was through embodying

---

25. Ibid., 35.
26. Ibid., 48.
27. Michael Downey, "Compassion," in *Dictionary of Catholic Spirituality* (Collegeville, MN: Michael Glazier, 1993), 192.
28. Nolan, *Jesus before Christianity*, 50.

misericordia that Francis and Clare invited others into this same restoration of one's full humanity.

With respect to the overall Christian tradition, usage of the classical Latin word *merces* (mercy) was gradually superseded by the word *misericordia* to refer to the act of showing kindness to those who have no claim, and from whom no requital can be expected.[29] Such was the condition of the leper, who would receive no alleviation from her or his suffering (physical, psychological, social) except from the compassion and loving kindness (*misericordia*) of others. If we associate this kind of compassion only with action, in the ways that the word "charity" is so often used today, we might conceptualize it as acts of "help," either of monetary or physical assistance. But the word "*misericordia*," by connecting a human response of the heart (*cor*) to a situation of misery, speaks even more deeply to an attitude and a relational disposition that comes from our inner depths—a courageous, generous "heartedness" that empowers us to make a difference in the lives of others.[30]

The restoration of the root word, "heart" (*cor*), to its cognate "courage" is critical because we tend to use the word "heart" sentimentally. But, as Rita Nakashima Brock reminds us,

> Heart, the center of all vital functions, is the seat of self, of energy, of loving, of compassion, of conscience, of tenderness, and of courage—the Latin *cor* means heart. To take heart is to gain courage. Our lives bloom in fullness from the heart, the core of our being, which is created and sustained by interconnection. Heart, used unsentimentally, carries rich connotations; it suggests powerfully the various holistic dimensions of self. Heart is the center, innermost region and most real, vital meaning and core of our lives. The human heart is symbolically the source of emotions, especially humane ones such as love, empathy, loyalty, and courage. The profoundest intellect lodges in our heart where thought is bound with integrity, insight, consciousness, and conscience. . . . Heart is what binds us to others, safeguards our memory, integrates all dimensions of ourselves, and empowers us to act with courage.[31]

29. See *Compact Edition of the Oxford English Dictionary*, vol. 1, s.v. "mercy."
30. Again, all of these observations about "mercy" being an impoverished and inaccurate translation of the concept of *misericordia* are recognized in Armstrong et al., *The Founder*, 534 n. b., which contrasts *miseratio*, an act of kindness, with *misericordia*, a heart sensitive to suffering.
31. Rita Nakashima Brock, *Journeys by Heart: A Christology of Erotic Power* (New York: Crossroad, 1988), xiv.

Thus, when Francis is describing the way of life that "the Lord gave him" as beginning when God drew him toward the lepers and he "showed compassion and loving kindness [*misericordia*] to them," we should understand Francis to be saying several critical things. First, the novelty of his loving impulse toward lepers, for whom Francis had previously felt disgust and contempt, was a singular and noteworthy act of grace within him. Because it empowered him to do something that he alone could not do, the impulse to *misericordia* was indicative, to Francis, of God's motion, God's desire, God's purposefulness acting within him. The wellspring of love surging within him and seeking connection with others was easily differentiable from Francis acting of his own accord. In that sense, we might call it grace. But we need to understand that this grace was not the operation of a foreign God coming in as a mighty power. It was a "quickening," a vital movement, drawing Francis into his humanity and asking him to join the rest of the human community. It was God coming alive, in and all around him—in a vital and living form of what the Christian tradition calls "incarnation." Francis's intuitive sense of God's love drawing him toward others was how he identified and recognized God coming alive in him. Further, he experienced, in that growing aliveness, the desire to share a life of dignity and joy within a community of love. The intense poverty and need of the lepers drew a new solidarity and a deeper generosity of spirit out of him, even as they taught him about the living God.

Leprosy reduced human beings to a single common denominator: debilitating terminal disease. The hopelessness of their circumstances drew Francis to offer them the little that he could: the reassurance and comfort of his personal presence. It wasn't as if Francis could cure them, nor even alleviate all that much of their physical pain. He could not even restore them to their homes and families. But his concern for their comfort and well-being, inside and out, could, in its own way, restore the dignity and connection to others that their illness, dependence, and marginalization may have diminished. It could also, to a small degree, make amends for the hardheartedness of others who were so willing to banish and ostracize them. And it was in that humble, basic, and simple space of repeated self-offering that Francis came to know God in the holiness of the authentic and sincere human-human encounter. But there was far more learning happening in the leper colonies than perhaps we have appreciated. It was in the leper colonies that Francis learned the power of love and the real truth of the gospel.

As Francis saw and experienced the living God in the discarded, he knew that the gospel was not a dead letter, nor was it only about the good news. For we cannot hope to revere God's good news if we fail to see God coming alive in one another. The quiet work of God in the human community *is* the good news, and living in communities of new life is the only real way we have of knowing the truth of resurrection. Love, hope, and the joy of sharing life together were turning spaces of death into vibrant communities where everyone belonged and everyone mattered. Far from some kind of utopian ideal or pious charity, these communities of *misericordia* were a prophetic witness to God's desire to come alive, to help us move from being merely human to being constantly humane, and to work together to build a world that is home for all. In committing themselves to the practice of *misericordia*, Francis, Clare, and the earliest Franciscan communities of men and women were learning together the intimate tenderness and steely strength of God's love in a profoundly new way.

In his reflections on Francis's life, Bonaventure calls Francis's engagement with lepers "deeds of humility and humanity." Thomas of Celano tells us that "[Francis] moved to the lepers and stayed with them."[32] The affection, kindness, and compassion that Francis learned

32. "From then on he clothed himself with a spirit of poverty, a sense of humility, and an eagerness for intimate piety. For previously not only had association with lepers horrified him greatly, so too did even gazing upon them from a distance. But, now because of Christ crucified, who according to the test of the prophet appeared despised as a leper, he, in order to despise himself completely, showed deeds of humility and humanity to lepers with gentle piety. He visited their houses frequently, generously distributed alms to them, and with a great drive of compassion kissed their hands and their mouths." Bonaventure, *Life of St. Francis*, 1:6, in Armstrong et al., *The Founder*, 534. Ewert Cousins's translation of Bonaventure's *Soul's Journey into God* notes that the Latin term *pietas* used here has a broader connotation than the English word "piety," encompassing "love, devotion, affection, reverence, kindness, fidelity, and compassion." See Bonaventure, *The Soul's Journey into God, The Tree of Life, The Life of St. Francis*, trans. Ewert Cousins

in the leper colony "transformed him into Christ"[33] through a "wonderful tenderness of compassion" in which "his soul melted for the poor and the infirm."[34] A thorough reorientation of his very personhood—a fundamentally new understanding of himself, his humanity, and his relationship with God and others, rooted in his experience of compassion in the leper colony—is the "way" that God gave Francis and that, at the end of his life, he prophetically bequeaths to us.

As I hope is already clear, it is important for us not to isolate Francis's contact with lepers to a single moment or incident in his life. Francis did not have a solitary encounter with a leper—although this is sometimes the way his story is retold, as if this new experience of God mediated through the leper was merely a spark of revelation in his life.[35] Loving solidarity with the outcast was the vital center of Francis's life. Much is made of how impactful his recognition of Christ in the leper was for Francis, and rightly so. But a careful reading of early Franciscan sources makes clear that Francis considered spending time in community with lepers to be an integral part of the formation process in the way of life he embodied. Thomas of Celano writes that after Francis and the early brothers received papal approval, they spent their days working "with their hands, staying in the houses of lepers or in other suitable places, serving everyone humbly and devoutly."[36] Another source indicates that "the brothers stayed in the leper hospitals," and "Francis used to call lepers 'Christian brothers.'"[37]

(Mahwah, NJ: Paulist Press, 1978), 250n1. Armstrong et al, *The Founder*, 586 n. a. refers readers to a lengthy article on the context of piety: André Méhat, Aimé Solignac, and Irénée Noye, "Piété," in *Dictionnaire de Spiritualité Ascetique et Mystique, Doctrine et Histoire* XII (Paris: Beauchesne, 1986), 1694–1743.

33. Bonaventure, *Life of St. Francis*, 8:1, in Armstrong et al., *The Founder*, 586.

34. Ibid., 589.

35. The story of Francis's initial encounter with a leper "while still in the clothes of the world"—that is, before his self-stripping before the bishop—is told in Thomas of Celano, for example, who adds it as something of an afterthought. In chapter 7 of his *First Life*, Thomas of Celano writes "The holy lover of profound humility moved to the lepers and stayed with them. For God's sake he served all of them with great love." Thomas of Celano sees the encounter with the leper as important in Francis's initial conversion process but not critical to Francis's identity. See Thomas of Celano, *Life of Saint Francis*, 1:7:17, in Armstrong et al., *The Saint*, 195.

36. Thomas of Celano, *Life of Saint Francis*, 1:15:39, in Armstrong et al., *The Saint*, 218.

37. *Mirror of Perfection*, 3:58, in Armstrong et al., *The Prophet*, 303.

Francis knew that there was a great deal more to learn about God and humanity by eating with, being with, and living with those whose vulnerability elicited in him a deeper appreciation of the sacred dimensions of human interaction. The "miracle" of Francis's conversion effected by ongoing relationship with lepers is not so much the change in his feelings from revulsion to pity or compassion but the slower miracle of transformation in Francis as he allowed himself to feel deep gratitude to them for all they taught him about himself, about being human, and about God incarnate. I think he was particularly grateful for how his friends in the leper colony invited him to grow as a person, especially in the areas of sensitivity, humility, and reverence. As the passage from Bonaventure's *Life of St. Francis* cited above suggests, this process transformed him by encouraging and reinforcing his ever deepening participation in the mystery of Christ's incarnation.

The *misericordia* learned in the leper colony was, of course, to be spread into the world, and here it is important to reiterate that this *misericordia* was multifaceted. Cultivating a genuine and human relationship with the marginalized involved growth in solidarity, empathy, compassion, humility, human vulnerability, and a sharper social and theological critique of the injustice and inhumaneness of marginalization itself. It is no wonder, then, that solidarity with sisters and brothers who were sick, impoverished, marginalized, or otherwise suffering was an integral part of the Franciscan way of life: not only was it a sharing in the care and concern that Christ manifested with his contemporaries,[38] it was also considered a fundamental foundation and orienting principle to our own humanity. Both men and women engaged in this way of life. Clare made provisions for sisters to serve outside the convent; she was not oriented to monastic enclosure as a value in and of itself, but only in so far as it supported the depth of prayer that her vision of *communio* required. While her *Form of Life*

---

38. What is traditionally called the "imitation of Christ" sometimes manifests in forms of piety; Francis and Clare's corrective to this tendency is to show us that the practical expressions of solidarity and love that Christ demonstrated are a *sine qua non* to any attempt to imitate Christ. Absent this transforming solidarity at the margins and in spaces of impoverishment, we might wonder if people are engaging a genuine imitation.

(the monastic rule she wrote for her sisters, the Poor Ladies) does not specify the kind of work that "ministering sisters" engaged in outside the convent, their presence in the community was meant to "constantly edify" others with virtue.[39] The sharing in a life of absolute solidarity with the sick, impoverished, and marginalized is explicit in the norms for daily life; for example, the Poor Ladies ate very sparingly, in solidarity with those who had nothing.[40] For women as well as for men of the early Franciscan movement, attending to the suffering bodies of their contemporaries proved to be an extremely important way of attending to the suffering body of Christ in the world and witnessing to the ongoing incarnation of God in humanity.

We are left to conclude, then, that the practice of *misericordia* was foundational to the Franciscan way of life, for women as well as men, and that this practice of *misericordia* entailed the prioritization of a relational experience of personhood over an egocentric one, with an intentional desire to affirm, support, and enhance the presence of God in our midst. Francis and Clare exemplified the power of tenderness by appropriating what they had learned about God's love and creating a loving way of being in human community. The earliest communities, at San Damiano and the Portiuncula, were experiments, then, in the daily practice of *misericordia* as taught by Christ. The assumption in those communities was that all would be continually growing in the tenderness and loving kindness that protects, sustains, and supports the presence of God in the human community. What would that look like?

Communities of Solidarity and Resistance

Three elements seem to be constitutive of the emerging Franciscan model of community: active care for one another, solidarity and *communio*, and prophetic resistance to injustice and sin. Before we examine those elements in the early Franciscan way of life, I would like

---

39. See *The Form of Life of Saint Clare*, 9:11–12, in Armstrong, *The Lady*, 122.
40. See, Ibid., 133. For other examples of radical solidarity with the poor, see ibid., 117–21: chapter 6 on not having possessions, chapter 7 on the manner of working, and chapter 8 on begging alms and the care of the sick.

to suggest that the Franciscan vision of community is a gift offered to the entire human community. From its inception through its historical development over the centuries, Francis's and Clare's experiences of the mystery of incarnation had universal implications for humanity that immediately challenged many cultural norms, but also intercultural and interreligious implications that continue to emerge as we ponder and dedicate ourselves to engaging the Franciscan vision. Certainly, their way of life is not limited to practicing Catholics or practicing Christians.

As Pope Francis now models so beautifully, Francis and Clare embodied the gospel's invitation to engage our human interrelatedness, our responsibility to one another, and the holiness that being human involves. This is, first and foremost, a human journey, one of universal solidarity, in which the "slow and arduous effort" of becoming a people requires "integration and a willingness to achieve this through the growth of a peaceful and multifaceted culture of encounter."[41] As Pope Francis states,

> Interreligious dialogue is a necessary condition for peace in the world, and so it is a duty for Christians as well as other religious communities. This dialogue is in the first place a conversation about human existence . . . a dialogue which seeks social peace and justice . . . in which, by mutual listening, both parts can be purified and enriched.[42]

For anyone with doubts about this, Pope Francis clarifies: "Evangelization and interreligious dialogue, far from being opposed, mutually support and nourish one another."[43]

We have suggested this already, but it probably bears reiterating: human community begins at the core, with our most intimate companions: those with whom we have actively chosen to be in community. For Francis and Clare, the new gospel way of life involved the formation of an intentional community that differed sharply from their families of origins. Forging relational ties with others who felt

---

41. Pope Francis, *Joy of the Gospel*, par. 220. Cf. Pope Francis, *Laudato Si'*, par. 14.
42. Pope Francis, *Joy of the Gospel*, par. 250.
43. Ibid., par. 251.

strongly called toward the demands of the gospel as Francis and Clare were exploring them was the locus of this early experiment in community, strongly influenced by ongoing engagement with the marginalized and the keen solidarity forged through vulnerability experienced in those communities. As we consider how we might incorporate elements of the Franciscan vision of community in our own relational lives, we would do well to integrate the element of intentionality in community formation as fully as possible. A caring community of solidarity and resistance forms because people want it to form, are ready and able to engage the inner changes that forming such a community will require, and because the community is able to self-monitor and call all of its members to greater integrity, maturity, and accountability. This is a community in which growth—individual, interpersonal, and social—is a primary, core value.

The element of choice in our configuration of intimate community is important; we speak of this as an "intentional community," which, while it may take many forms, will always have a significant commitment, on the part of each member, to grow and to choose toward "what better leads to God's deepening life" in us and in our connectedness. As Parker Palmer explains:

> The core of the Christian tradition is a way of inward seeking that leads to outward acts of integrity and service, acts of love. Christians are most in the Spirit when they stand at the crossing point of the inward and the outward life. And at that intersection, community is found. Community is a place where the connections felt in our hearts make themselves known in the bonds between people and where the tuggings and pullings of those bonds keep opening up our hearts.[44]

Palmer urges us to consider community as a process as much as a place, writing:

> Community is another one of those things (like personal well-being) that eludes us if we aim directly at it. Instead, community comes as a by-product of commitment and struggle. It comes when we step forward to right some wrong, to heal some hurt, to give some service. Then we

---

44. Parker Palmer, *The Promise of Paradox: A Celebration of Contradictions in the Christian Life* (San Francisco: Jossey-Bass, 2008), 90.

discover each other as allies in resisting the diminishments of life. It is no accident that the most impressive sense of community is found among people in the midst of such joyful travail, among those who have said no to tyranny with the yes of their lives.[45]

Relationships that explore and embody *misericordia* and *communio* constantly renew interpersonal commitments at emotional, physical, and spiritual levels and extend that same loving graciousness in relationship to others. It is in this way that we begin to live in the reality of discovering and nurturing human goodness and giftedness in one another. Rita Nakashima Brock describes this process well:

> Good is grounded in our deep awareness of others, our willingness to participate in mutual transformation, the expansion of quality, the increase of meaning that comes from increasing connectedness, and the deepening of communion among all who participate in relationship. . . . The good that includes but moves beyond our own individual existence to become sacred emerges from the risks each of us takes to be vulnerable to relationships. Mutual support, intercommunication, and sensitive openness, the only avenues of divine power that create good, require enormous risks.[46]

Because there are both risks and responsibilities that are an integral part of such a community, there are also built-in assumptions about personal maturity, commitment to ongoing personal growth, honesty, integrity, and sensitivity to the growth process in others. Not everyone is willing and able to commit to the principles and even ground rules that are necessary for the healthy functioning of such a community.[47]

---

45. Ibid., 80–81.
46. Brock, *Journeys by Heart*, 47–48. This characterization of community emerges toward the end of her analysis of the intersection of human interconnectedness and divine incarnation. Her description of the potentiality of human connection is a development of the thought of Henry Nelson Wieman's arguments in *The Source of Human Good* (Carbondale: Southern Illinois University Press, 1967).
47. In other words, members of a functional, intentional community must be "ready, willing and able," and each of these adjectives is necessary. There are some who are willing, even desirous, of community life in some form but unable, for a variety of reasons (emotional, physical, psychological), to fulfill the commitments necessary to being a vital and functioning member of the community. There are others who are "unready"—for example, lacking in self-knowledge, not prepared or not open to the demands of empathic engagement of others—for such a commitment. Again, because such commitments are not easily "legislated," an important element in the fundamental health of the community is to be wise and discerning about how the ethos, ideals, and principles of the community are communicated, assessed, "enforced" (if and when necessary), and grown in each person over the lifetime of the community. The health, well-

As should also be clear, such a community does not materialize on its own; it requires each individual's commitment to nurturing and sustaining both one's own well-being and the well-being of the community as a whole.

The community that Francis and Clare strove to build was not accidental but rooted in the intentional practice of *misericordia*, as we defined it above. Such a community, in which interpersonal "communion" deepens over time, takes dedication and commitment to the human potential we glimpse, through the love of God, in ourselves and others. The graceful, grace-imparting love of God is the foundation of such a community; it is not merely a human work. And yet God alone does not "make" such a community happen. Active, adult collaboration is necessary. We draw from the generous wellspring of God, in our depths and in our midst, taking both inspiration and vitality from the source of life that God's love is. Those who have not experienced this form of interpersonal relationship or *communio* may believe that it is ethereal, "fuzzy," even impossible, a belief that an overly sentimental or emotional definition of love fosters. However, there are critical elements to relationships rooted in true *communio*. They are known by and through their power to awaken us to a deeper sense of purpose, to instill wisdom in discernment (i.e., the capacity to make wise and sensitive choices, both individually and collectively), to encourage sensitivity to the promptings of the spirit of God, to grow in courage as prophetic witnesses to a more just way of being, to inspire and provide the vision for individual and collective transformation necessary within structures of suffering and injustice, and to console and galvanize the human community at large as we take heart and draw strength from one another. To see the potential embedded in our own humanity unleashed, growing and flourishing in ourselves and others, is intrinsically joyful, mysterious, and inspiring.

Because it is both intentional and mysterious, it would be unreasonable and unwise to "expect" or "demand" that such a grace-

being, and growth of each individual must also be encouraged and supported. As we think about "sustainability" in our world today, these elements of personal, interpersonal, and communal "maintenance" should form a part of our conversations.

filled process be an intrinsic part of every relationship or community. Experience shows us that only some relationships can nurture the flourishing of our deepest personhood. Our review of the early lives of Francis and Clare and the violence that each of them experienced within their own familial contexts should caution us that we will not always be blessed to experience or learn such sacred and life-giving love in our own households, friendships, or intimate relationships.[48] Whatever our familial history, all of us will surely have to grow into adult forms of the love that gives life and create the best community context to embody that love in the larger world. For Francis and Clare, saying "yes" to the love of God required a whole new context of relatedness and familiarity; it demanded a certain "no" to their families of origin with all of their expectations, as well as to many if not most of the social and cultural norms of their day. The community they created was the foundation of the gospel life they sought to practice. Living out the daily practice of "showing *misericordia*" in the practice of tender care toward one another made it possible for them to extend this practice out into the world at large.[49]

For Francis and Clare, cultivating an intense and fervent love for all that is good, in the world and in others is not a "soft" love that tolerated anything, but rather one that could love the suffering and disenfranchised even as it could simultaneously admonish and call to accountability those who contributed to oppression. It is instructive and somewhat lost in our traditional retellings of the Franciscan story that both Francis and Clare understood their way of life as primarily a way of penance—a way that they themselves followed and that they

48. For a profound and highly relevant discussion of this reality, see Brock, *Journeys by Heart*, 1–24, esp. 16: "Because the very existence of heart is basic to the structure of human life itself and is the basis of our being broken in relationships, we require connections if we are to acknowledge our own broken heart and be healed. At the earliest part of our lives we are dependent on the loving power of others to nurture us. Their failure to do so has serious consequences. We are broken by the world of relationships before we are able to defend ourselves. It is not a damage we willfully choose. Those who damage us do not have the power to heal us, for they themselves are not healed. To be healed, we must take the responsibility for recognizing our own damage by following our hearts to the relationships that will empower our self-healing."

49. See Thomas of Celano, *Life of Saint Clare*, 19:2 commenting on the intensity of Clare's prayer: "She opened more generously the depths of her mind to the torrents of grace that bathe a world of turbulent change."

preached to others, by word and example. Doing penance is a direct response to sin; without personal and social sin, penance would be unnecessary. Francis and Clare intended their way of life to lovingly invite people away from the patterns of sinful behavior that trapped them and oppressed others.[50]

How should we understand this way of penance? It is a way of constant conversion, rooted in doing all that needs to be done to continue to uphold, protect, defend, and support human dignity. Love, rooted in true solidarity with another, demands justice. When one takes the lived reality of another seriously, appreciating the challenges that the other experiences and wanting them to know the encouraging love of God, a keen sense of the other's dignity and worth emerges. That Francis, Clare, and their early companions were sensitive enough to the injustices of their world to preach a prophetic form of conversion to the gospel demands of justice often gets lost when we speak of the love that they tried to embody in the world.

Franciscan scholar Michael Cusato calls this essential Franciscan insight "the universal fraternity of all creatures, especially those most difficult of creatures: human beings," and, as he explains, this insight is the key to understanding the entirety of Franciscan theology. Because all are brothers and sisters to one another, Cusato writes,

> everything that breaks the bonds of this sacred human fraternity created by God—through the destructive and abusive use of power, through the placing of oneself over and against others for the private advantage of one to the disadvantage of others—is what, for Francis, constitutes sin. Moreover, to understand what Francis means by sin is to understand what he means when he says that he began to "do penance." "To do penance" is to distance oneself from all those actions and attitudes that threaten to rupture the bonds of the human fraternity.[51]

50. Francis called his early movement the "brothers and sisters of penance." And although his life encompassed massive change and conversion, he never lost his sense of being caught up in a web of sin, needing constant healing, light, and remediation. In fact, the opening statement in Francis's Testament, "The Lord gave me, Brother Francis, thus to begin doing penance in this way," reflects his insight that the human condition never entirely escapes sin, and, because of that, penance is always necessary. See Francis of Assisi, Testament, 1, in Armstrong et al., The Saint, 124. Clare begins her Testament, as well, in the context of this way of penance: "The most high heavenly Father saw fit in mercy and grace to enlighten my heart that I might do penance according to the example and teaching of our most blessed father Francis." See Clare of Assisi, Testament, 24, in Armstrong, The Lady, 61.

As Cusato makes clear, the penitential preaching of Francis and the early Franciscans is a prophetic denunciation of all that "ruptures the bonds" of human communion, of human solidarity, friendship, and collaboration—in other words, it is a denunciation of all human activity that does not revere and honor the dignity of the human person.

That some in his own religious community refused to enter the leper colony and therefore denied the Christ who was so palpably real to Francis there only makes Francis's *Testament* all the more poignant. His statement to his brothers of "the way that the Lord gave me" can now be read as an urgent plea that they follow this way of *misericordia* that Francis learned from Christ through the leper colony: "Go there," the subtext might read, "and engage your relationship with those who suffer marginalization and the contempt of the world. You will find God there, and be drawn into the mystery of God-become-human, God experienceable somehow in the midst of our own human community."

Francis's *Testament* should be considered a "corrective" to the order's incorporation of any number of compromises to absolute poverty, not just materially, but socially and even theologically. In other words, Francis recognized that it was not simply the virtue of poverty that was at stake. More fundamentally, the quality and depth of his brothers' experience of God was eroded by their aversion to the God made known in and through the marginalized, a God Francis had first come to know in the leper colony, and who had revealed to Francis so much, about Francis himself, about the core of our humanity, about the mystery of God enfleshed. In addition to being an admonition of sorts, we should consider Francis's *Testament* to reflect his desire to share his experience of God with others, a desire that only grew over the course of his life as an extension of his embrace of genuine poverty. As his self-stripping increased, the only and truest "thing" he had left to share with anyone else was his experience of God and his desire to embody the generous love of God that he had experienced. Thus, the habit of *misericordia* gave rise to the practices of *communio*, inviting

---

51. Michael F. Cusato, "Of Snakes and Angels: The Mystical Experience behind the Stigmatization Narrative of 1 Celano" in *The Stigmata of Francis of Assisi: New Studies, New Perspectives* (St. Bonaventure, NY: The Franciscan Institute, 2006), 70.

others to participate and share in the unitive life, the mystery of God-with-us.

Because God had communicated to Francis, through the powerless, a new vision of community, he became keenly sensitive to the abuse of power as the root cause of sin. Renunciation and denunciation of power—all forms, at least, of power in which power was wielded over others rather than used to invite and accompany the less powerful to well-being—was, therefore, a critical element in Francis's conversion to God through the leper. The gospel that Francis and Clare and their earliest companions were preaching was a radical message of love that hoped and strove and worked for the betterment and deepest well-being of others, upholding the dignity of all God's creation. Francis and Clare understood that the human community, created by God in God's own image, is inherently sacred. As Christians, they understood that, in Christ, all humans are made one, and therefore that all are brother and sister to one another. Francis's famous Canticle of Creation, in which he extols the elements of nature and calls them "brother" and "sister," extends this sense of communion into all of creation.

*　*　*

The immediate problem in identifying love as the heart of the new gospel life that Francis and Clare created is that we have no real context—cultural, religious, emotional, or even theological—for understanding and appreciating the depths of this love or its demands upon us to ensure and uphold human dignity in the face of forces that daily assault it. Concurrently and as a direct corollary, we have yet to explore the capacity of tenderness to empower us into a new way of being that facilitates human growth toward gospel principles in action. Indeed, in some ways, our own impoverishment, as individuals, communities, and even as a species, is rooted in our inability to be capacitated and revitalized physically, emotionally, intellectually, and spiritually through the dynamic power of love. Our understandings and experiences of power are so deeply entrenched in forms of power that are demonstrated by force or coercion that we have been cut off from our own inner sources of power, reflecting the inadequacy of our concepts and paradigms of both love and power. I recognize that in tying, conclusively and inextricably, Francis and Clare's gospel vision to the cultivation and manifestation of divine love as an incarnate dynamism that radiates through humanity, many will immediately judge that I have "softened" the academic or theological rigor of my analysis, opting for the sentimentality of the heart, for an "affective spirituality" that floats ethereally above the challenges of life in the here-and-now. But if that is so, it is already a sorry statement about the shortcomings of our intelligence as a species and how we define "intelligence" and affectivity in narrow, ultimately self-defeating ways. It could well be that our very survival depends upon a fundamental shift in our theory and praxis of love and power.

Thus, I follow Francis and Clare in challenging us, as I believe Christ did, to take the power of love seriously, placing all of our other resources as human persons—intellect, creativity, insight, wisdom, passion, wit, humor, etc.—in the service of the only vessel strong enough to integrate, temper, and direct our giftedness in ways that have the possibility of enhancing our well-being. In this sense, I am also attempting to be as faithful to and authentically representative of the Franciscan and the Christian tradition as I know how. If the fundamental insight of Christianity is that God is love, then there must be a power to that love that we have yet, as humans, to fully appreciate or enact in our own lives. If love, for us, "waters down" and sentimentalizes life instead of energizing, revivifying, and empowering us—in short, if love does not make us wiser and more intelligent—then surely we have missed the gospel message, the same gospel message that Francis and Clare sought, wholeheartedly, to convey to their contemporaries. Love gives us a perspective on humanity that we can gain in no other way except through our openness to the power of love. As we collaborate with God and with others more actively in love, a radical new way of being human is forged. That love is a power that can dissolve, undo, and reconfigure all other forms of power is a reality that most of us would prefer to deny than to engage, particularly because it would change every other assumption or preference —intellectual, social, political, theological—that we have.

So let us return to the now-familiar terrain of Francis's conversion process—first the leper colony and then the public self-stripping—and view it afresh. When Francis gave his father back his clothing before the bishop, it is easy to see that as a renunciation of his wealth, his inheritance, his patrimony. It is perhaps less obvious for us to see that it was a radical renunciation of power and autonomous identity. By renouncing his social status and access to wealth, Francis is not only "nakedly following the naked Christ," he is asking God for a new identity, an identity that is not rooted in power over others but in the richness of his relationships with God and others, experienced qualitatively in terms of the intensity of connectedness and the transformative impact of that union. As Francis had already instinctively realized, the path toward this new identity was best learned through the *misericordia* he had experienced among lepers and the outcast. For the *misericordia* he had begun to learn with lepers had already taught Francis more about power than his experiences of war, wealth, popularity, and social acceptance, which he had found came at a cost to his humanity. But what he found in the leper colony was an enhancement of his humanity—a new richness that he experienced in and through his humanity because he found a connection to others and to his deepest personhood. Wisdom and insight into the incarnate reality of God and the communion that God's love makes possible within the human community were central to that new identity as a human person. The core texts that both left behind—Francis's *Testament* and Clare's letters to Agnes (which we will explore in the next chapter)—should be seen as documents that reflect their role as mentors offering counsel, solidarity, encouragement, and inspiration in a new way of life. They are an invitation into a fuller experience of the mystery of God within the dynamics of our own communities.

The way of *misericordia* has many implications about how power manifests and expresses itself in human relations. In addition to being instructive about gentleness, compassion, and tenderness, this way invalidates the use of power to dominate, abuse, or injure another's dignity, even as it allows for the use of power to protect, defend, and advocate for human dignity and right relations. In theory, of course, Francis and Clare wanted to live in communities in which it was not necessary to impose discipline but rather where each member of the community freely embraced the values of the community and therefore needed mentoring, accompaniment, support, and counsel rather than much active coercion, remonstrance, or discipline. In so far as they had to legislate, they tried to do so clearly and simply, as in the following examples:

> And let no one be called "prior," but let everyone in general be called "lesser brother." And let one wash the feet of the other.[52]

> Let them love one another, as the Lord says: *This is my commandment: love one another as I have loved you.* Let them express the love they have for one another by their deeds, as the Apostle says: *Let us not love in word or speech, but in deed and truth.*[53]

> Likewise, let all the brothers not have power or control in this instance, especially among themselves; for, as the Lord says in the Gospel: *The rulers of the Gentiles lord it over them and the great ones make their authority over them felt; it shall not be so among the brothers.* Let whoever *wishes to be the greater among them be their minister and servant. Let whoever is the greater among them become the least.*[54]

At a practical level, Francis appeared to want to use power over no one. Having come to a deep sensitivity to the sacredness of communion as the root of all relationality, exerting power over another likely felt like a violation of the inherent holiness rooted in the relationship. By the end of his life, if we are to believe Thomas of Celano's *First Life*, Francis wanted nothing more than to "return to serving lepers and to be held in contempt, just as he used to be."[55] Francis was grieved, toward the end of his life, that the popularity of his movement had actually neutered the radical inversions of power that had first signaled, for

52. Francis of Assisi, *Earlier Rule*, 6:3–4, in Armstrong et al., *The Saint*, 68.
53. Ibid., 72.
54. Ibid., 67.
55. Thomas of Celano, *Life of Saint Francis*, 2:6:103, in Armstrong et al., *The Saint*, 273.

him, the authenticity of his experience of God and that had formed a critical part of the early Franciscan identity. It was profoundly dispiriting for Francis to experience that those who aspired to follow Christ according to the way that Francis believed God had revealed to him refused the very basic premises of the path of *misericordia*—a way of poverty and solidarity that enriched one's experience of one's own humanity.

It is significant that, after so much conflict and turmoil over how to proceed as a religious order, Francis felt compelled to make a final statement, calling those who professed loyalty to his way of life back to the place where his own journey had begun: the simple, raw, and holy experience of God's love known and shared in and with the lepers. In his *Testament*, Francis reveals his concern that his movement was already drifting away from the gospel's radical demand for justice and loving kindness to the marginalized and oppressed. Francis knew *misericordia* as a call to create communities of solidarity and resistance, communities capable of resisting evil, in its multitude of forms, and supporting and upholding right, loving human relations. He and Clare can teach us how to nurture and cultivate such *misericordia* in our daily lives. From them we learn that only a love that is "stronger than death" will have the wherewithal to confront abusive power, protect the innocent, and prevent trauma and violence from dividing the human community. How will we sustain and nurture that depth of love?

5

Cultivating Tenderness: The Ground of Our Belonging

Image 5a. The courtyard of San Damiano.

The gentle and deep peace of the church of San Damiano makes it seem an unlikely epicenter of loving activity. And yet that is what it is. This is the church where Francis was said to have understood God asking him to "rebuild my home." This is where Clare and the community of Poor Ladies settled as the movement grew. This is where Francis returned to recover after his forty days of prayer and fasting culminating in the stigmata at La Verna. This is where he wrote his famous Canticle of the Creatures, which so deeply inspired Pope Francis's encyclical *Laudato Si': On Care for Our Common Home*. This is where Clare spent forty years of her life, praying and providing necessary gravity to the apostolic work of the Franciscan movement with her contemplative life, which we can glimpse through her letters to Agnes of Prague and the witness of her sisters in community, the Poor Ladies. The entire Franciscan story derives its deepest roots from this place, living roots that give us insight into the vital core of a love capable of grounding a revolution of tenderness.

For love to grow, it must be rooted and grounded in a community oriented to cultivating and nurturing the growth of all of its members. We have already seen elements of the kind of growth we are talking about: growth in integrity, in maturity, in wisdom, courage, honesty, solidarity, and love. In the previous chapter, I suggested that no single quality could capture the meaning of *misericordia*, but that it was best understood as the antonym to hardheartedness. In this chapter, I will attempt to articulate some of the relational practices, traditionally understood as prayer and contemplative practice, which give us eyes to see the world and others around us from a space of loving connection. It is this contemplative stance that grounds the *communio* that Francis and Clare embodied with others and that many continue to seek today.

For some people, contemplation connotes a particular temperament they think they do not have. I do not know the number of times people have told me, "I am not a contemplative; I don't have that kind of patience" or "I wouldn't know how to begin to meditate." But if we think of contemplation as an expression of love—an expression that grows more intelligent, patient, and tenacious because it proceeds from an even deeper knowledge that we are loved—then perhaps we can begin to see contemplation for what it really is: a practical, living, empowering, transforming way of life that supports and energizes us at all levels of our being. This is an inborn capacity that gets trained out of us by a world that tells us how we should think, how quickly we should make decisions, what should inform our thought processes, tripping us up by sending us a multitude of conflicting messages about what is attractive, necessary, desirable, and important. Contemplation helps us to stay accountable to our own capacities, our wounds, and our need for discipline in order to grow.

Contemplation is, first and foremost, a disposition, a willingness to engage a process, to change and be changed. Whatever our background, we can probably appreciate the multiple benefits—to ourselves, to the people we love, and to the world around us—that contemplation offers. A contemplative person is one who never stops asking "what is real?" The converted, contemplative person values simplicity, integrity, and relational honesty so much that nothing else really matters to them. This clarity about what truly matters to them manifests itself in courage, calm, warmth, and vitality as their inner access to radical love radiates outward. A contemplative community brings wisdom, discretion, inspiration, and visionary leadership into the world. Like Jesus and his earliest companions, such a community nurtures growth and calls us to be accountable to the impulses that stir us toward the common good. Contemplation is less about leaving the world and more about becoming real. As more of us dedicate ourselves to the process of becoming authentically ourselves and sharing our giftedness with others, the world becomes a different place. Because contemplation is a relational orientation, it helps us continually evolve the forms of tenderness that Francis and Clare inspired and nurtured.

Contemplation is a holistic engagement of the will, heart, and mind that, in practice, becomes a way of life. Contemplation is, emphatically, not merely a practice, although the practice is critical in order to develop the mind, heart, eyes, and ears to see, hear, savor, behold, and attend to what is most real in the world around us. Contemplation gives us the capacity to see what is as well as what is not yet and the strength to work toward all that wants and deserves to be. Contemplation is not an individual process but a relational one: it is an integral part of the process of falling in love with the One whose love is beyond all telling. No one can fully embrace a relationship with God without contemplation. The contemplative process, Clare promises, invites us into a transforming relationship as we literally begin to see God.[1] Clare's second letter to Agnes of Prague, written in 1235, offers us an elegant encapsulation of that process in the form of four verbs: gaze, consider, contemplate, and imitate.[2] Taken together, these verbs express elements of a relational activity that builds intimacy and fuels transformation. Both Francis and Clare's regular intimacy with God was what enabled their extraordinary tenderness with others; that intimacy sensitized them to God's constant presence in the human community and empowered them to work courageously to make a fitting home for God and for all in the world around them.

Engaging more deeply in our relationship with God is inherently transformative, helping us to reshape our priorities, values, daily practices, and capacity to see ourselves and our world anew. We are changed as a direct result of engaging the profound power and mystery of the God who is an eternal outpouring of love that creates, sustains,

---

1. Cf. Clare of Assisi, *The Third Letter to Agnes of Prague*, 12–14, in Armstrong, *The Lady*, 51:

> Place your mind before the mirror of eternity!
> Place your soul in the brilliance of glory!
> Place your heart in the figure of the divine substance
> And, through contemplation,
> transform your entire being into the image
> of the Godhead itself,
> so that you too may feel what friends feel
> in tasting the hidden sweetness
> that, from the beginning,
> God Himself has reserved for His lovers.

2. Clare of Assisi, *The Second Letter to Agnes of Prague*, 20, in Armstrong, *The Lady*, 49:

> Most noble queen,
> gaze,
> consider,
> contemplate desiring to imitate Your Spouse.

and ultimately draws all things back into Godself as the very source of their being.

Francis and Clare believed that this reality—that God is always at work within creation simply because God is love and has loved all things into being—was (is) our deepest reality, and it is not so much an effort of faith as an exploration of genuine relationship that allows us to experience this as our daily reality. The core of Francis and Clare's desire was to invite people into the mystery of God's love through what they did and, more importantly, through who they were—or rather, who they had become over the years of embracing relationship with God. They modeled, mirrored, and offered to us the possibility of living in and living out the love of God. And they did so selflessly, by example, preaching the gospel at all times and using words when necessary. Their legacy—the teachings that they leave us—are in themselves nothing less than revolutionary. But their revolution is not meant to remain merely textual. Like Jesus, they invite us to experience the God who is at the center of our being and who walks with us out of the margins of our own existence.

We have already seen that one of the most primary insights of the Franciscan way is that human life is meant to be deeply relational. By "relational," we mean that life is best lived in solidarity and communion with one another and with God. The most critical relationship, of course, is the relationship that exists between the individual and God, a relationship that concurrently invites us into a deeper, more holistic relationship with ourselves and others. It is likely that, like Francis, we begin the transformative process of contemplation with little true self-knowledge. And so the gaze becomes an important way to see our deepest reality despite the darkness in the world around us. For we grow into the reality of a loving relationship—with God, self, and others—gradually and in small steps: awareness, experience, joyful sharing, moments of insight, gratitude for all that is gained in encounter, sorrow for the ways that we fall short, desire to be there for the other in trustworthy and helpful ways. All of these experiences lead to a gradual letting go of lesser ways of being and can propel a whole-hearted embrace of a new and increasingly compelling reality. Sustained practices of presence (of bringing the whole of ourselves into moments of encounter—again, with God, self, and others) make it possible to live in this new way.

Noting that prayer is, as Teresa of Avila described it, "nothing more than conversation with One whom we know loves us,"[3] we see that Francis engaged a trusting familiarity with God, even when he hardly knew who God was. If we go back to one of the critical moments in Francis's own conversion, we can hear again his profound prayer before the cross of San Damiano as the starting point of a life-long conversation:

Enlighten the darkness of my heart.
Give me a right faith, certain hope, and perfect love,
with deep humility, wisdom and understanding,
that I may know and do Your most holy will.

We can all relate to this prayer of a person who just needs help; if we are honest, we will admit that we all start right here. Francis's words are a simple and humble recognition that the human heart is fundamentally mysterious; elements of our selves remain hidden and "dark" to us, and many of the human trials and tribulations we face are exacerbated by our lack of deepest self-knowledge.[4] As Francis had already become aware by this time in his life, an honest prayer for illumination was necessary if he was going to know himself and embrace the way of life God might intend for him. We can see in this prayer that, just like us, Francis had no idea where the God of his heart would lead him. Surely he often returned to this humble request for guidance as his questions about how best to live out God's will for him increased.[5]

---

3. See Teresa of Avila, *The Book of Her Life*, 8:5.
4. See Teresa of Avila, *The Interior Castle*, 4:1:9. The Fourth Dwelling Places, or fourth stage of Teresa's seven-stage journey toward union with God, describe the task of integrating humility, self-knowledge, prayer, and experiences of revelation. For more extensive commentary on this stage in the spiritual life see Ahlgren, *Entering Teresa of Avila's* Interior Castle, 49–59, esp. 53–54.
5. Although Francis's *Testament* does not use the language of "enlightenment" explicitly, we have seen that he starts it by saying, "The Lord gave me, Brother Francis, thus to begin doing penance in this way," suggesting divine inspiration and guidance.

"Enlightenment," of course, is a journey and a process—all of the world's mystical religious traditions teach this. Even a piercingly profound moment of revelation, should we ever be privileged to experience one, is only a small piece of a much larger, painstaking process of moving from the obscurity of "now," in which I see only partially, to the "then" of gradually "seeing face to face."[6] Thus, Francis's prayer to "enlighten the darkness of my heart" can be seen (and could even serve us today) as a simple mantra, repeated over and over as a daily intention to continue to turn over what is "dark" (i.e., puzzling, mysterious, challenging, or even frightening or disgusting) to us into the light of God, that we might learn from it whatever God would teach us and continue, in this way, to grow in wisdom and grace and goodness.[7] This intention to learn from all that life hands us helps transform even that which most challenges us into something that will cultivate a deeper relationship with God.

As Francis grew in his relationship with God, we see many instances of both the spontaneity and constancy of his prayer life, suggesting that he enjoyed a deep and rich intimacy with God. *The Legend of Three Companions* states that Francis's attraction to prayer began after his return to Assisi following his experience as a prisoner of war in Perugia. The text specifically correlates an inner feeling of intense tenderness with these moments of prayer, which began in the same sudden way as Francis's initial experience of God in the leper colony:

> Suddenly he [Francis] was visited by the Lord who filled his heart with so much tenderness that he was unable to speak or move. He could only feel and hear this marvelous tenderness; it left him so estranged from any

6. 1 Corinthians 13:12: "For now I see as through a mirror dimly but then I shall see face to face." This text is one of the core scriptural texts used to describe the unfolding mystery of the mystical life. Franciscan theologian Bonaventure, for example, makes use of it at the outset of his mystical treatise *The Soul's Journey into God* as a way of inviting his readers into the progressive journey toward God, writing: "Enter into yourself, then, and see that your soul loves itself most fervently; that it could not love itself unless it knew itself, nor know itself unless it remembered itself, because our intellects grasp only what is present to our memory. From this you can observe, not with the bodily eye, but with the eye of reason, that your soul has a threefold power. Consider, therefore, the operations and relationships of these three powers, and you will be able to see God through yourself as through an image, which is to say *through a mirror in an obscure manner.*" Bonaventure, *Soul's Journey into God*, trans. Cousins, 80.

7. Cf. Luke 2:40.

sensation that, as he himself said later, even if he had been completely cut to pieces, he would not have been able to move. . . . From that very hour he began to consider himself of little value and to despise those things which he had previously held in love. . . . Often, almost daily, he withdrew secretly to pray. He was inclined to do so by that same tenderness he had tasted earlier, which now visited him ever more frequently, driving him to prayer in the piazza and in other public places.[8]

His actual forms of prayer were quite simple and straightforward, always reflecting humility and a strong desire to be shown, led, drawn toward what would best manifest what God wanted from him. He sought out lonely places where, in quiet, he might better hear God's guiding voice. We also know of several instances when Francis asked God a specific question and opened scripture three times to allow the word of God to speak to him directly.[9] He enjoined Clare and other trusted companions to pray for and with him as he discerned God's will for him over the course of his life. He was devoted to the Eucharist and meditated on scripture. He composed and sang hymns of praise. He maintained an attitude of gratitude and love in the face of a wide range of human responses to his lifestyle. Through consideration of these regular features of Francis's life, we can confidently posit a deepening dialogue with God, with and beyond words, that gradually became what we could call the unitive life.

But these individual habits in and of themselves do not help us understand, in a more "inner" way, the process by which Francis's life gradually became a single, whole, and seamless integrated prayer. Francis's prayer practice was fervent, physical as well as mental, and continuous, embedded into the fabric of his life. Bonaventure's poetic language describes Francis's constant prayer in ways that help us to see prayer as relational activity, an intensifying process of seeking and being found, a relationship that continually punctuates daily life. Bonaventure writes:

8. *The Legend of Three Companions*, 3:7–8, in Armstrong et al., *The Founder*, 72.
9. See, for example, Thomas of Celano, *Life of Saint Francis*, 2:2:91–93, in Armstrong et al., *The Saint*, 261–3. Bonaventure also describes this practice as a prefatory part of his stigmatization experience at La Verna. See Bonaventure, *Soul's Journey into God*, 13:2, in Armstrong et al., *The Prophet*, 631.

Francis strove to keep his spirit in the presence of God by praying without ceasing lest he be without the comfort of the Beloved. . . . Whether walking or sitting, inside or outside, working or resting, he was so focused on prayer that he seemed to have dedicated to it not only whatever was in his heart and body, but also all his effort and time.[10]

Although Francis's prayer life seems to have evolved to a place in which he often experienced moments of absorption in which the intensity of encounter with God suspended his ordinary activity, it was truly his perseverance in engaging contact and relationship with God that fueled his life. "Distrusting his own effort and trusting divine piety, prayer was a fortress to this worker; for in everything he did, he cast his care completely upon the Lord through his perseverance. He firmly claimed that the grace of prayer must be desired above all else."[11] And again Bonaventure describes:

He usually neglected no visitation of the Spirit. Whenever it was offered, he would follow it; and for as long as the Lord granted, he enjoyed the sweetness offered. . . . Many times he was suspended in such an excess of contemplation, that he was carried away above himself and, experiencing what is beyond human understanding, he was unaware of what went on about him.[12]

As Francis progressed in prayer, it became inseparable from the fervor of his love, as Bonaventure notes, "The unconquerable enkindling of love in him for the good Jesus had grown into lamps and flames of fire, that many waters could not quench so powerful a love."[13] As this text suggests, for Francis, as for Clare, prayer and love were a single act, a single force, a single impulse, extending itself gracefully into every facet of daily life.

If we had to summarize what prayer was, for Francis, we would be on very safe ground asserting that Francis made continual recourse to his relationship with God not only by means of "conversation" but also in wordless embodied ways that actuated the promise of Christ in

---

10. Bonaventure, *Life of St. Francis*, 10:1, in Armstrong et al., *The Founder*, 605.
11. Ibid.
12. Ibid., 10:2 in Armstrong et al., *The Founder*, 606.
13. Ibid., 13:2 in Armstrong et al., *The Founder*, 631.

the Gospel of John that those who love Christ and keep his word will know the indwelling presence of God.[14] Cultivating and maintaining an appropriate inner dwelling place for God so that we might alternately rest in that presence and share it with others is a foundational part of the apostolic and evangelical life. The process of becoming a dwelling place for God sacralizes our experience of self, other, and world; as we "begin to understand ourselves as dwelling places of God, we can then take more seriously the possibility that our life, our selfhood, and our relationships with others are all sacred spaces to be cultivated."[15] Creating an inner space for the indwelling presence of God was so important that Francis implored his companions to prioritize above all else the practice of loving and adoring God as simply and wholeheartedly as possible, writing in his *Rule*:

> But, in the holy love which is God, I beg all my brothers, both the ministers and the others, after overcoming every impediment and putting aside every care and anxiety, to serve, love, honor and adore the Lord God with a clean heart and a pure mind in whatever way they are best able to do so, for that is what God wants above all else. Let us always make a home and a dwelling place there for the One Who is the Lord God Almighty.[16]

Creating a dwelling place for God, a suitable home—in our hearts, our communities, and our world—for the One whose love gives life, is at the very core of the gospel way. We participate in the making of places sacred as we attend to the presence of God that already dwells there and as we open ourselves to our own graced capacity to be vessels of that presence in our world. To put it another way, sacred space is "determined primarily by a spiritual attitude towards space and towards what it contains." Gathering intentionally in loving community helps to create a sacred space, and Francis modelled the kind of reverence that recognized the human person as "the *locus* of the Spirit . . . the Holy Place of the encounter with God."[17]

14. See John 14:23. On this passage and the image of the human person as the dwelling place of God, see Gillian Ahlgren, *Enkindling Love: The Legacy of Teresa of Avila and John of the Cross* (Minneapolis: Fortress Press, 2015), 17–22, and Ahlgren, *Entering Teresa of Avila's* Interior Castle, 21–28.

15. Ahlgren, *Entering Teresa of Avila's* Interior Castle, 24.

16. Francis of Assisi, *Earlier Rule*, 22:26–27, in Armstrong et al., *The Saint*, 80.

17. Steven J. McMichael, "Francis and the Encounter with the Sultan (1219)" in *The Cambridge*

Our culture of encounter needs a grounding, a communal space that we sacralize deliberately with our orientation to hospitality, compassionate care for others, prayer and reflection, cultivation of simplicity, and purity of heart. In many ways, Clare's entrance into the Franciscan story allowed the evolving charism of Francis's earliest community to settle and take hold. The space of San Damiano was pivotal. There Clare had the cross that had called Francis to "rebuild my home" as a concrete reminder of God's loving invitation to change and be changed. For Clare and her sisters, the daily practice of gazing on that cross, especially when enhanced by communal prayer, scripture reading, Eucharist, and participating in the care of others, reinforced the many ways that they were sustained and fed by the living God. Clare was convinced through her own experience that in gazing into the mirror of the cross, we see and receive God's self-giving love, a revolutionary experience that changes all aspects of our lives. Over time, Clare's sustained awareness of the incarnate God ceased to be located in any single place as she felt and experienced the reality of God's effective presence in her and in all of humanity. Steven McMichael describes a similar experiential process at work in Francis when he considers Francis's experience of prayer and his stigmatization at La Verna, writing:

> What is also unique is that the space that became sacred was not just the mountain in Tuscany but the very body of Francis. The human person becomes the *locus* of the cross, which is the only thing, along with their infirmities, that human beings can glory in (*Admonition* V). The holy sepulcher, honored by Christians as a reminder of Christ's passion, death and resurrection, loses importance when it is compared with the real place where these events are effective, namely, within the human being. Francis's writings testify to his belief that the human being is the bearer of the divine. Therefore, greater attention should be placed on the human person—body, soul and spirit—than on spatial things.[18]

In ways that should be instructive to us today, Francis and Clare model

Companion to Francis of Assisi, ed. Michael J. P. Robson (Cambridge: Cambridge University Press, 2012), 138.
18. Ibid., 139.

for us how to become more aware of and attuned to God's active presence in humanity. They teach us that genuine prayer requires us to grow. Their prayer was not sentimental or self-serving. It was never demanding or transactional. In voicing their deep desire to be in synchronicity and union with God's desire, their prayer left the world tangibly better off.

Clare's fourth and final letter to Agnes of Prague, full of rich, spousal imagery, reflects her deep intimacy with God. Written shortly before her death in 1153, the letter makes clear that Clare's prayer life had become as "natural" as the act of breathing. Although she describes a form of prayer ("Gaze upon that mirror each day . . ."), a steady life of forty years of contemplative living had provided Clare the supportive embrace of the one

> Whose tenderness touches,
>> Whose contemplation refreshes,
>> Whose kindness overflows,
> Whose delight overwhelms,
>> Whose remembrance delightfully dawns.[19]

Embedded repeatedly throughout this letter are references to the life of the bride in the Song of Songs. Clare clearly experienced the joy, longing, and fruition of love as an integral part of daily life. She urges Agnes (and, we can assume, all of us) to grow into the fullness of an identity as God's cherished partner when she writes:

> May you, therefore, be inflamed ever more strongly with the fire of love! As you further contemplate God's ineffable delights, riches and perpetual honors, and, sighing, may you cry out from the great desire and love of your heart:

> Draw me after you,
>> let us run in the fragrance of your perfumes,
>> O heavenly Spouse!
> I will run and not tire,
>> until You bring me into the wine-cellar,
>> until Your left hand is under my head

---

19. Clare of Assisi, "Fourth Letter to Agnes of Prague," 11–12, in Armstrong, *The Lady*, 55.

and Your right hand will embrace me happily,
You will kiss me with the happiest kiss of Your mouth.[20]

Clare's mature theological vision suggests that a profound, vibrant, and fertile love relationship with God incarnates itself within us and, through us, in the larger world around us as we gradually enter into the living experience of God through Clare's simple method: gaze, consider, contemplate, imitate. As we gaze, we see the love of God extending itself toward us, inviting us into a new understanding, both of who God is and who we are. Gazing, as a practice and as a relational invitation, is not something that remains between us and God. Gazing becomes a way to engage others and the world around us: lovingly and with the desire to dwell together and bring the best out of one another. For to gaze is not simply to see; to gaze is to be drawn into the one we see.[21]

To gaze is to behold rather than to scrutinize and examine; it entails a particular attitude, disposition, and presence in us that is well worth exploring because our contemporary culture has stripped us of the practice of the gaze. The visual images that surround us, many of which are violent or pornographic, have dissociated our eyes from our hearts and minds, which threatens to make our gaze superficial, voyeuristic, crude, and, certainly, unloving. Forging a holistic relationship with what we see and learning to behold what is within us and around us is part and parcel of the practice of the gaze—a practice that we may not even know how to engage.

The art of gazing is a form of true beholding. The gaze, by definition,

---

20. Clare of Assisi, "Fourth Letter to Agnes of Prague," 27–31, in Armstrong, The Lady, 57. The lined exhortation contains four references to the Song of Songs (1:3, 2:4, 2:6, and 1:1). In commenting on this letter, Ilia Delio asks us to consider the "youthful spirit of joy" manifested in Clare's exultation in the love of God, especially in light of the fact that, when she wrote this letter Clare was nearly sixty years old and had been bed-ridden for a good part of her life. Delio notes: "Clare writes her final letter to Agnes as if in the youth of her spiritual life. She is filled with hope, love and desire, as if she has just discovered the source of happiness, the pearl of great price. . . . It is . . . a lifetime of gazing [on the crucified Christ] that generates in Clare the Spirit of confidence in the love of God and the spiritual transformation of her own life into the image of Christ." Ilia Delio, Clare of Assisi: A Heart Full of Love (Cincinnati: St. Anthony Messenger Press, 2007), 97–98. And: "Even at the end of her life when she was sick and frail, her spirit showed the lightness of a youth in love." Delio, Clare of Assisi, 100.

21. Cf. Delio, Clare of Assisi, 30.

involves a disposition of reverent attention and tenderness of heart. This more open stance predisposes us to be able to learn from what we see, to be in relationship with what we see, to be transformed by what we take in from the gaze. The act of gazing is an act of the heart through the eyes, not of the eyes alone. The mind attends, too, but in reverent silence, there to ponder rather than to dissect through analysis. If we have spent enough time in nature beholding creation and natural beauty, this practice is more natural to us. The gaze opens up a space in us to meet and be met in a transforming encounter, to share mutually in another's genuine presence, and this practice is critical, both for our relationship with God and our relationship with one another. Rainer Maria Rilke captures some of the dynamic of how our practice of beholding transforms us and others when he writes:

> I know that nothing has ever been real
> without my beholding it.
> All becoming has needed me.
> My looking ripens things
> and they come toward me, to meet and be met.[22]

As we bring our tenderness of heart and our full attention to the cross of San Damiano—a cross that neither emphasizes nor ignores suffering, reflecting more prominently the kind eyes and loving embrace Christ extends into the world—we may begin to sense the open arms of God, who comes to us there, to meet and be met.[23] Clare asks Agnes (and

---

22. Rainer Maria Rilke, *Rilke's Book of Hours: Love Poems to God*, trans. Anita Barrows and Joanna Macy (New York: Riverhead Books, 1996), 47. In the previous stanza, Rilke describes both the delicacy and power of such a moment, which captures all of our senses:

> The hour is striking so close above me,
> so clear and sharp,
> that all my senses ring with it.
> I feel it now: there's a power in me
> to grasp and give shape to my world.

23. It is worth repeating for emphasis, particularly if you are not familiar with the details and countenance of the San Damiano cross, that it conveys many subtleties. Delio notes helpfully: "The San Damiano cross that Clare gazed upon does not depict a lonely, abandoned figure of Christ but a crucified-glorified Christ surrounded by a community of disciples." Delio, *Clare of Assisi*, 34. The figure of Christ is ringed with women and men, as well as angels supporting and upholding his body. The archangel Gabriel and Mary at the moment of the annunciation frame his hands. The San Damiano cross communicates the simple and pure love that joins heaven and earth freely, gracefully, eternally.

us) to gaze upon the cross as in a mirror because that gaze of loving kindness helps us to know ourselves inwardly, to glimpse and engage who we can become. Once we are graced with the vision of ourselves that God gives us, that same gaze can open in us the desire to become that person, in partnership with the One who calls that personhood out of us. This deepening happens as we engage the second verb in Clare's four-step method, "consider."

Consideration brings reflection into the process and helps us to integrate the intellect with the heart from a loving space of greater focused attention. Consideration refines the gaze by centering it in a space of single-mindedness, setting aside anything that can alter or weaken our gaze in order to integrate intellectual, not just affective, attention on it. Consideration helps us both to add a process of knowing to the gaze and to correct some of our lesser forms of knowing through the eyes of the beholder, whose stance is one of love and who aspires to greatest wisdom. From this integrated space contemplative engagement, the third step, can emerge.

If contemplation, as Roch Niemier claims, "requires a radical shift in thinking," then the previous two steps of gazing and considering foreground this shift, so that we can gain the relational perspective that contemplation provides. "Deep contemplative prayer," Niemier writes, "is not so much learning how to contemplate God by some method or practice, as it is becoming aware that it is God who is contemplating us."[24] Here is the corrective to our worry that prayer or contemplation is something that we have to accomplish (and that we are unable to do very well). If prayer is truly God praying in us, then contemplation is the awareness, consent, and participation to the aliveness of God in us. Contemplation is the grounding for us to learn how to collaborate with the divine in every facet of our lives. Contemplation is the space in which we learn not only God's aliveness but God's desire to make us partners with God in the work of making the world a better place. In this sense, there is no true tension between contemplation and action. The contemplative life moves toward

24. Niemier, In the Footsteps, 117.

prophetic action, and the active life craves the contemplative grounding that is so necessary for apostolic witness.

The fourth verb in Clare's process, "imitate," brings this point home. For imitation does not mean to mimic the behavior of another. As Roch Niemier develops this term, he explains that

> when Clare used the term, she was asking Agnes to become the image of the God on whom she gazed. . . . Imitation is transformation insofar as Christ comes alive in my life. In this transformation contemplative union happens. . . . As we give ourselves over to the truth of "God contemplating me," God's gaze of love over the course of years transforms us and empowers us. Eventually, God slowly recognizes God's own image in us. It is important to think of this process in terms of relationships and the holy mystery of growing in love. I personally am not sure anyone can truly pray without being in love.[25]

What Niemier helps us to see is that we ourselves are transformed in large part because we now actively engage a relationship that empowers us. This relationship gives us a unitive grounding such that we have access to a strength and a source of wisdom beyond ourselves. This contemplative, relational grounding gives us the capacity for purposeful action in the world around us:

> When we look at prayer this way we become not only transformed but empowered, and being so empowered, we are able to work to effect the necessary changes in ourselves, in life, and in society and the world around us. God works in union with us, in union with our spirit, not apart from us. It is a matter of working at life together.[26]

The scriptural and theological grounding for the four steps of this process, as Clare outlines it, is the image of God in which we are said to be created (Gen 1:26–27) but that has been clouded over, perhaps even effaced, through our estrangement from God. Engaging that relationship with God, guided by Christ's instructive example of human potentiality and empowered by the living spirit of God, creates a space for the indwelling presence of God that Francis had exhorted his

25. Ibid., 118–20.
26. Ibid., 120.

followers to seek: "Let us always make a home and a dwelling place . . . for the One Who is the Lord God Almighty."[27]

The invitation into the divine embrace may well take some time for us to acknowledge, understand, accept, and integrate. The images we have of God—whether they emphasize severity and judgment, mystery and remoteness, ethereality and transcendence, or power, grandeur, and majesty—may keep us from entering into a realm of intimacy, familiarity, gentleness, creativity, and genuine partnership and collaboration with God. And here is where Clare's language of *speculum*, often translated "mirror," is so helpful. For an English equivalent of the medieval Latin *speculum*, we need to consider not only the outer reflection that is offered to us as we gaze but also the inner knowledge of what we see in the reflection. A *speculum* reflects back to us our inner reality. It is used to see inwardly, and it helps us to see not only what is real and true inside us but to apprehend the meaning and subjective, transforming truth of that inner reality.[28] If we gaze on the cross, seeing and receiving the inner, subjective reality of God's love there, we can be invited into the reality of the divine embrace, the mystery of God's total self-giving. And as we give ourselves over to that reality, we want nothing more than to mirror back that total self-giving, in the glorious exchange of mutual, life-giving love. The poetry and exultation of Clare's fourth letter to Agnes, with its regal and spousal overtones, are a small but telling echo of that exchange that goes far beyond what words can say.

Henri Nouwen opens the reality of God's rich love for us in a way that may be easier for us to appropriate today. In *The Life of the Beloved* he writes:

> The unfathomable mystery of God is that God is a Lover who wants to be loved. The one who created us is waiting for our response to the love that gave us our being. God not only says: "You are my Beloved." God also asks: "Do you love me?" and offers us countless chances to say "Yes." That is the spiritual life: the chance to say "Yes" to our inner truth.[29]

27. Francis of Assisi, *Earlier Rule*, 22:27, in Armstrong et al., *The Saint*, 80.
28. Cf. Mueller, *Clare of Assisi*, 40–42.
29. Nouwen, *Life of the Beloved*, 133.

But this ongoing dialogue between us and God is not merely personal. God's love, alive in us, is a counter-cultural force, as Nouwen continues:

> The spiritual life counteracts the countless divisions that pervade our daily life and cause destruction and violence. These divisions are interior as well as exterior: the divisions among our most intimate emotions and the divisions among the most widespread social groupings. The division between gladness and sadness within me or the division between the races, religions, and cultures around me all find their source in the diabolic forces of darkness. The Spirit of God, the Spirit that calls us the Beloved, is the Spirit that unites and makes whole. There is no clearer way to discern the presence of God's Spirit than to identify the moments of unification, healing, restoration, and reconciliation. Wherever the Spirit works, divisions vanish and inner as well as outer unity manifests itself.[30]

* * *

So it is a whole new understanding of self, of God, of the world that gradually opens up for us through the gaze of love, but this understanding is in no way abstract. It is a life-giving, transformative understanding, a "saving knowledge" taken lovingly into the whole of our being, such that we are left changed, different, enhanced, and empowered by it—empowered for joy, empowered for new life, given a new sense of purpose, a true reason for being here on earth. How can it be otherwise if gazing is actually also an experience of "tasting the other, of taking the other into oneself,"[31] if gazing is our response to the invitation of scripture to "taste and see" the goodness of the Lord? As Clare so beautifully expresses it, in the process of this gaze, we "taste the hidden sweetness that God has reserved for those who love God."[32] Clare's way shows us that the "gospel life" is not grandiose or exaggerated, either in its leadership or in its servitude. It eschews pageantry. It is a simple and humble and joyful creation of a dwelling place for the divine—the making of a space for God's presence, in our hearts, our homes, our communities, and our troubled world.

The constancy of the demands of our world requires our dedication

30. Ibid., 135.
31. Delio, *Clare of Assisi*, 32.
32. Clare of Assisi, "Third Letter to Agnes of Prague," 14, in Armstrong, *The Lady*, 51.

to sustaining the gaze and allowing the insights gained there to inspire us to right action. The gaze is a living, dynamic experience of God that we take into ourselves and live back out into the world. In our hearts, our bodies, our homes, and our communities, this lived relationship with God takes form and shape and more concrete expression. Thus, as we participate more actively in the gaze, we become part and parcel of the ongoing incarnation of that living and dynamic experience of God, making it more "real" to our contemporaries, modeling and putting into practice the possibility of deeper partnership and collaboration with God, that the love of God might be made more manifest in our world today.

An integral part of the gaze itself is sustaining it, which is far more difficult to do than we might think, particularly when the messages of the world around us strongly contradict what we take in through the gaze of God's loving kindness. Our definition of the gaze as our core practice of prayer, then, must include the ways that we position ourselves so that we can sustain the gaze. There are too many things—in ourselves, in our lives, even in our families and communities (the intimate spheres of our lives), much less in our world—that can easily and powerfully get in the way of the gaze. We must be attentive to this vulnerability in us and in the human condition at large, not allowing things that contradict the loving intent of God's gaze to detain us, in any way, from our seat right there at God's side, wrapped in the embrace that shows us who we are.

This principled commitment to sustaining the gaze is perhaps all the more important as we are learning the practice of the gaze, for there is so much to learn and apprehend and integrate through the gaze that it deserves our dedication. Much of what orders our lives may well begin to show signs of inadequacy or falsity in comparison to what comes to us through the gaze of God's love, and it is worth remembering that Francis and Clare gave up all they had in order to approach God's gaze simply and nakedly. It is for God to show us the new norms of our life-in-God, and this will likely result in tremendous adjustments on our part. Our culture all but demands that we conform to lives that lack deepest joy, vitality, and love. And sometimes we ourselves settle into joyless lives, talking ourselves into it with a twisted sense of what we "should" be doing. My own sense is that such spiritual self-deprivation comes from our not lifting up everything to God in prayerful conversation and taking our cues about all of the details of our lives directly from the sacred, unitive space of the gaze. I am always heartened when I remember Teilhard de Chardin's simple indicator that we are on the right path when he writes: "Joy is the infallible sign of the Spirit of God."

Our lives, because they are human, will contain experiences and events that disrupt the gaze and perhaps even threaten to dislodge our engaged apprehension of the divine. Approaching God from a space of inner poverty—one in which we come without trying to force an outcome or bring too much with us into the space of encounter—helps us return to whatever inner or outer struggles we are experiencing in our lives with greater clarity and purpose. Ilia Delio captures the interdependence of poverty and the gaze well when she writes:

> Gazing requires a space within the heart to receive what we see and to "embrace" what we see. Poverty helps create this space because when we are free of things we possess or that possess us we are able to see more clearly and to receive what we see within us.[33]

That the things we possess can "possess us," as Delio says above, doesn't always occur to us. But this was precisely the insight that propelled Francis and Clare into their way of life. Through them, we can more easily see that so often our lives in the material world have holds on us that we do not appreciate. We gain a far greater freedom to make choices toward the deeper flourishing of our lives and our relationship with God in the engaged space of the gaze. The gaze of God that we sustain is not just given for us alone. We must be faithful and attentive to it and to the cherishing love that it teaches us, sustaining the gaze so that we can learn to gaze upon ourselves and gaze out upon others and the world in the same loving ways that we are being taught.

33. Delio, *Clare of Assisi*, 31.

We might conclude by suggesting that the gaze is a "movement toward." A movement toward God, toward the authentic self, toward the image of God embedded within us and, through the creative process, within all that God loved and loves into being. While its context is silence and reverence as we behold, the gaze itself is not passive. It is a holistic movement of the heart—an impulse of love within us made possible by the impetus and embrace of God's love, which empowers the heart to "'open its arms,' so to speak, to allow the Spirit of God's love to enter."[34]

What happens to us, in us, when the spirit of God's love enters our hearts? If we sustain the gaze, we can see things in an entirely new way. We see with clarity. We can see ourselves as God sees us—potentially free of that which hinders us and keeps us from knowing and manifesting the image of God within us. We can also see, within ourselves and within humanity, the habits, practices, and beliefs that keep us from growing toward that image, mired down instead and engaged in lesser, false ways of being. This clarity enkindles a greater resolve within us and a deeper prayer for the grace to change our ways. We can see the natural world around us, alive and glowing not only with beauty but also with the light of God's love embedded within it. We develop a stronger desire to live compatibly and companionably with the natural world, in ways that sustain its beauty and spontaneous generosity. And we are overwhelmed by the generosity of love we continually discover in the God who extends this love into as much of our being as we will allow. Gradually this generous, spontaneous, humble, and joyful way of life becomes part and parcel of who we are, just as it did for Francis and Clare.

"We are created to express the Word of God in our lives," Delio asserts. "In fact," she continues,

without striving for such a goal, we remain incomplete and lost, ambivalent, restless and anxious. What Clare calls us to is not something other than what we are but rather what we truly are created to be—icons of Christ. Christ lives in us and becomes our life when we come to live

34. Ibid.

our true identity (or self) in God. To put on Christ is to allow God to take root in our hearts and put on our flesh, not hiding God in the little pockets of our hearts but rather allowing the grace of God to shine through our lives—fragile and weak though they may be.[35]

For both Francis and Clare, "life in God was a perpetual deepening of union in love." Their example invites us to explore God's invitation to us to be drawn ever more deeply toward the infinite source of love. Delio writes that "Clare's movement toward God connotes a type of perpetual ascent, being drawn by the infinite love of God toward happiness, fulfillment and immense joy. There is light and levity in her pursuit of holiness, as if each discovery of God's immense love is a new beginning."[36]

The practice of the gaze fuels a process of transformation that leaves no part of us untouched, unchanged. While it takes place in the inner depths of our hearts, it is a transformation that completely redefines how we see and relate to ourselves, the world, and one another. As we linger in the gaze of God's love, we slowly create a deeper space for God's indwelling presence in us and in our world. This is a personal and intimate process for each of us, as we slowly apprehend that we are lovable (whether or not we have been well loved in our own lifetimes), that we are made for love, by love, and that we are meant to share that love with others. Taking this reality into ourselves, we find, perhaps to our surprise, that we have literally fallen in love, and the practice of the gaze helps us to stay in love for the rest of our lives. I am privileged to see this process of "falling in love" happen to people, over and over, as I lead pilgrimages to Assisi and as we approach the gentle space of San Damiano and proceed deeply into the heart of La Verna.

Acquiring a growing familiarity with God's love may not be quite so common an experience for all of my readers. Throughout this chapter, I have been speaking about God's love as if it means something to you, and yet it might be that you have never really considered that love in a deeply experiential and holistic way. It would be a tremendous

35. Ibid., 72.
36. Ibid.

disservice to all that I have been privileged to witness over the years, both in myself and in others, to leave what I have written about God's love in some abstract realm. If God's love is not yet, for you, a subjective reality, it occurs to me to ask you the question that no one has ever asked me and that the process of writing about the gaze has required me to ask of myself: "What does God's love feel like to you?" After that question came to me, I had to recognize how terribly odd it felt to me that, despite my training not only in theology but also in pastoral care and counseling and spiritual direction, and my years in spiritual direction as a directee myself, no one had ever asked me that particular question. We talk all around it, perhaps, getting one another to "notice God's presence" in our lived experience, but we rarely have a conversation with someone about our actual and direct experience of God's love, a living, transformative reality that, as we come to trust it, makes all the difference in our lives.

Staying in subjective contact with God's love—recalling it when our senses are dulled and doing all we can to maintain the living flame of love in our hearts—is an essential part of the journey of life. It is well worth our time to consider what God's love feels like to us—the familiar qualities of it, as well as all of its textures and nuances—and to let it become our point of reference and identity. The ways that God's love has been expressed, even "delivered," to us over the years, with exquisite precision and a profound knowledge of what we deeply need and deeply desire. Reflecting on our experience of God's love helps us to recognize the constancy of it, even in moments of confusion and struggle. Likewise, engaging the process of the gaze at San Damiano helps us to become more aware of the constant embrace of God, offered to us directly as well as in the beauty of creation and in the tenderness of intimate contact as we gaze upon others and notice how they, too, can communicate God's loving presence to us. I would like to close this section of my reflections by returning to the passage on love attributed to Pedro Arrupe, former minister general of the Society of Jesus (Jesuits). Arrupe's Ignatian sense of the call to "find God in all

things" resonates with the radical concreteness of the mystery of love
that Francis and Clare experienced and embodied.

Nothing is more practical than finding God, that is, than falling in love in
a quite absolute, final way. What you are in love with, what seizes your
imagination, will affect everything. It will decide what will get you out of
bed in the morning, what you will do with your evenings, how you will
spend your weekends, what you read, who you know, what breaks your
heart, and what amazes you with joy and gratitude. Fall in love, stay in
love and it will decide everything.[37]

*   *   *

*San Damiano is one of the most peaceful places on earth. It is the heart of
the Franciscan charism, and to pray there is a great privilege. Francis built
it by hand, stone by stone, as his first act of self-consecration to God. Then
he lovingly turned it over to Clare and the Poor Ladies as the movement to
"rebuild my home" took human form. The place still breathes the holiness of a
sincere and prayerful heart. One of the greatest joys is to arrive there very early
in the morning; one is entranced by the birds, the natural beauty, the simple
mystery of a new day.*

*On pilgrimage, I place our visit to San Damiano at least halfway through
our week, after we cover together the material presented in this book so far. In
other words, by the time we experience San Damiano, we have already moved
through the drama of Francis and Clare's conversion and their commitment
to poverty, simplicity, and a gospel-centered way. We turn to San Damiano
to explore what life on the other side of all that renunciation really feels
like—what it means to live in* misericordia, *the tender love of God.*

*We always walk there, usually in silence. The way down to San Damiano
from the city center gets narrower and more peaceful with each step. Passing
through the city walls and crossing the road that rings the city, we enter the
shimmering grove of olive trees, and, about halfway down the hill, there is
a circular area of benches. We pause to read Clare's fourth letter to Agnes
of Prague and reflect on the core of her teachings on contemplative prayer,
encapsulated in her counsel:*

37. "Fall in Love," *Ignatian Spirituality.com* accessed August 30, 2016 at http://www.ignatian
spirituality.com/ignatian-prayer/prayers-by-st-ignatius-and-others/fall-in-love.

> Most noble Queen,
>> gaze,
>>> consider,
>>>> contemplate
>>>>> desiring to imitate Your Spouse.[38]

When we arrive at San Damiano, we proceed directly into the chapel where we follow the counsel of Clare: just gazing at the cross, with "a quiet attentiveness, simply being open to the wonderful presence of God with no words, no thoughts, just being there."[39] This contemplative gaze of love invites us into "a relationship that changes us over the course of time . . . the prayer that allows God to pray within us so as to draw out what is best in us and speak to us in loving personal terms, so that we go away from prayer a transformed person and we discover in ourselves the image God has always wanted us to be." Delio concurs, writing: "Contemplation is a way of seeing the depth of something that leads to union with what one sees. . . . In [so] seeing, we enter into the mystery and become united with what we see."[40]

It is not all that hard, through that contemplative gaze of love, to begin to think differently about the words Francis first heard here: "Francis, rebuild my home. Can't you see it's falling into ruins?" And to see that this invitation was not only about rebuilding the church of San Damiano itself or even the church, more broadly, as a structure and an institutional body but also, and most primarily, about the "reform," the "rebuilding" of ourselves. The remaking, body and soul, of each one of us, individually and communally into a human family in a common home, in a deep communio *rooted in love.*

If we are the living stones of the church, if our bodies are temples of the Holy Spirit, and if somehow, in our totality, the human faithful make up the body of Christ in the present moment, then the call to "rebuild my home" might well mean reclaiming the holiness of God in our midst—within ourselves

---

38. Clare of Assisi, "Second Letter to Agnes of Prague," 20, in Armstrong, *The Lady*, 49. This four-fold process is discussed in many works on Franciscan spirituality, including Ilia Delio, *Franciscan Prayer* (Cincinnati: St. Anthony Messenger Press, 2004).
39. Niemier, *In the Footsteps*, 116. The cross that hangs in the chapel of San Damiano is not the original. After Clare died (1253) and her body was moved up to the church of San Giorgio (which consequently became the basilica of Santa Chiara upon her canonization in 1255), the community of Poor Ladies was moved up to a Proto-Monastery next to San Giorgio and the original cross of San Damiano went with them. It hangs in the side chapel of the Basilica of Santa Chiara.
40. Delio, *Clare of Assisi*, 56.

as individuals and in our communio. Honoring, revering, nurturing, and sustaining the presence of God in ourselves and in our midst.

Francis and Clare help us to move deeply into the heart of what "community" truly means. By teaching us so eloquently how to love—how to love God passionately, in one another and in ourselves as well—they invite us, through love, into a new way of being. A new way of being human, a new way of being us, and a new way of interacting with others, of being in a relationship, of being a people. In their radically simple way, Francis and Clare show us that what we call "church" or "religion" or "spirituality" is nothing more or less than the desire to be loving, put into daily practice in the prayerful cultivation of a reverential life. By searching for God in true poverty—of body and of spirit—they found deepest freedom and joy in going right straight to the heart of things—to the very heart of God.

Time at San Damiano encourages a deeper trust in the possibility of the mystical life, not as some abstract ideal for saints but as a way of life open to each of us—a way of life that would bring far more vitality and joy than any other way of life we could embrace. "We are created to express the Word of God in our lives," we read; we are asked to "allow God to take root in our hearts and put on our flesh, not hiding God in the little pockets of our hearts but rather allowing the grace of God to shine through our lives—fragile and weak though they may be."[41]

The gaze into God we gain at San Damiano makes that completely believable.

41. Ibid., 72.

6

Manifesting Tenderness: The Invitation
for Today

Francis and Clare had an intuitive sense of God's presence in the world around them. They had experienced that presence in the poverty and need of others; they had felt the inherent dignity and worth of the human person, and they shared God's desire to be more fully and intentionally incarnated in all of human life. They worked toward the most authentic manifestation of divine love in the world, understanding its capacity to transform people and therefore the ways of life that breed exclusion, disparagement, violence, and degradation in the human community. Because, like Jesus, they lived at the margins in poverty and radical solidarity, their knowledge of the human condition moved them to align the human community more clearly with the changes necessary if we are going to create a community where everyone belongs. They embodied God's presence by ridding themselves and their communities of any barriers that might hinder love's capacity to reach and transform others. Their shared sense of God's immense love released an energy into the world through the frail but powerful channel of human presence. The Franciscan tradition works as powerfully as it does and is as authentic as it is and speaks as compellingly as it does because it was built upon a shared dream, a shared vision, co-created by two pure and loving people working hand in hand with others who shared their passion to make the world a fitting place for all of its inhabitants to share life, with God and with one another.[1]

Many of us today share that dream. Especially when we are honest about our current failure to live together well. What Henri Nouwen has said so beautifully about community in the small sense ("Instinctively, we know that the joy of life comes from the ways in which we live together and that the pain of life comes from the many ways we fail to do that well."[2]) is true both in our spheres of intimate relations as well as in our current global situation. If we were truly honest about the state of our world today, its global inequities, the levels of violence and instability, and the situation of the displaced, the hungry, the isolated and abandoned, how many of us could take real pride in it? In fact, the urgency and uncertainty of our global reality calls us to engage the genius of Francis and Clare in our world today as we recognize the truth of Pope Francis's assessment: "We require a new and universal solidarity."[3]

As Francis and Clare teach us, solidarity is rooted in transforming encounters that give God a chance to speak to us through the challenges of our time and the poor who show us God's face. It is through our common humanity that the incarnate God comes to meet us and to free us from the unworthy chains of an individualistic, indifferent, and self-centered mentality in order to "attain a way of living and thinking which is more humane, noble and fruitful, and which will bring dignity to our presence on this earth."[4] Encountering God in the desperation of our sisters and brothers and finding, in their stories, points of entry into our own humanity is gripping, compelling,

---

1. We need only recall the appeal Francis made to others: "Let us always make a home and a dwelling place for the One Who is the Lord God Almighty." See Francis of Assisi, *Earlier Rule*, 22:27, in Armstrong et al., *The Saint*, 80.
2. Nouwen, *Life of the Beloved*, 89–90; see above, p. 44n21.
3. Pope Francis, *Laudato Si'*, par. 14.
4. Ibid., par. 208.

and exactly what Pedro Arrupe was trying to capture in his poem about falling in love and staying in love. The love that gives meaning to our lives is revealed to us as we discover that we have the capacity to be there for others, to be there with others in their space of deepest need. As Alan Jones helped us to understand what happened to Francis when he first discovered God in the leper colony: "This God is no hobby."[5]

Francis and Clare's genius was their adherence to poverty and simplicity in order to commit themselves wholeheartedly to the love of God that life at the margins made real and concrete. This focus, lived out daily in communion with God, whose love subsequently empowered the outpouring of love they offered those around them, epitomized the experience of Christ and his closest friends and gave substance and flesh to the love of God. Both of them were uncompromising in their focus on the naked Christ known in our poverty and precariousness, particularly Clare, who labored over forty years and with four popes to ensure that the "privilege of poverty" would allow her community the freedom to pursue radical solidarity with the incarnate God in a completely undistracted way.[6]

If we hold their refusal to compromise in creative tension with their tenderness, perhaps we will approach Francis and Clare's invitation to us today. They invite us to commit to upholding the holiness of humanity without compromise. This means that every time we see a case of marginalization, oppression, or suffering, we defend human dignity. Every time we see greed, exploitation, corruption, or violence, we hold one another accountable and demand change. They invite us to a greater intentionality in how we live together. They ask us to become a community of mutual accountability in which we scrutinize our assumptions and behaviors, aligning them with the demands of justice, dignity, and peace. Where there is blindness, stubbornness, or contempt for what is holy, this community does not hesitate to

---

5. See above, p. 45.
6. See Mueller, *Privilege of Poverty*, esp. 33–52. Cf. Bernard McGinn, *Flowering of Mysticism*, 43: "Francis' originality rests in the totally uncompromising way in which he tried to fulfill what it meant to follow the crucified Christ by witnessing to the gospel of the world."

"correct in love," denouncing all that dehumanizes us and challenging us to reconsider behaviors and systems that exclude or oppress.

In more explicitly Christian terms, they challenge us, like Jesus, to grow constantly toward greater magnification of the *misericordia* of God. This community is one that always has "room at the table." It is welcoming, with special attention to those who have suffered or been trampled down. However, it is and also should be uncompromising. This is not an easy love feast. Respect for the dignity of those around the table requires mutual self-discipline and personal maturity. And there will always be some who do not want to sit at such a table, as Albert Nolan reminds us:

> The "kingdom" of God, then, will be a society in which there will be no prestige and no status, no division of people into inferior and superior. Everyone will be loved and respected, not because of one's education or wealth or ancestry or authority or rank or virtue or other achievements, but because one like everybody else is a person. . . . Those who could not bear to have beggars, former prostitutes, servants, women and children treated as their equals, who could not live without feeling superior to at least some people, would simply not be at home in God's "kingdom" as Jesus understood it. They would want to exclude themselves from it.[7]

Recognizing the call of God toward a process of deeper human authenticity, integrity, fidelity, and abiding love, we must create and sustain communities of solidarity and support that will help us uphold, revere, defend, and protect the presence of God in the world around us. We must make a decision to live as sisters and brothers, sharing life together. This way of life helps us to become "capable of seeing the sacred grandeur of our neighbor, of finding God in every human being, of tolerating the nuisances of life in common by clinging to the love of God, of opening the heart to divine love and seeking the happiness of others. . . . We are called to bear witness to a constantly new way of living together in fidelity to the Gospel."[8] The church that results is a church that "lives the truth in love,"[9] able to offer "a radiant and

---

7. Albert Nolan, *Jesus before Christianity* (Maryknoll, NY: Orbis, 1992), 71–72.
8. Pope Francis, *Joy of the Gospel*, par. 92.
9. Cf. Eph 4:12b–16: "Building up the body of Christ until we all attain to the unity of faith and knowledge of Christ, to mature personhood, to the extent of the full stature of Christ, so that we

attractive witness of communion," modeling kinship, care, and what it means to be friend, sister, and brother to one another, and causing admiration in "how you care for one another, and how you encourage and accompany one another."[10]

Francis's recognition of the presence of God in the human person and the graceful work, with God and others, to nurture holiness in the human community is what made him who he was. His reform, of church and of community, rested in that dedication to human dignity, and it is instructive to us, whether or not we are Catholic, whether or not we are Christian. With respect to the church of his own time, Francis saw the foundational reality of the presence of God as an invitation to all people in the church, hierarchy included, to reexamine and reconsider their lives at every moment, so that they might constantly follow, more truly and more authentically, the Christ whose presence on earth had given humanity a new view of itself. Through his way of life, Francis sought to offer a nonhierarchical way of being a church to the entire people of God. What he mirrored back to those in positions of authority was the presence of Christ throughout the entire church, particularly in those surprising spaces of poverty and abandonment, where one might assume Christ was absent.

It is clear that Francis viewed institutional allegiances for their own sake as deeply problematic. Under increasing pressures to "institutionalize" his own community as its membership expanded, Francis deliberately withdrew from a position of power even as he continued to believe that his lived witness of poverty and simplicity should serve as a primary and authoritative form of charismatic leadership. The situation of Clare is perhaps even more instructional than that of Francis. As a woman, Clare was in even less of a position to negotiate the terms of her religious life than Francis. Enclosed and often ill, she could not meet with officials who decided her own future and

may no longer be infants, tossed by waves and swept along by every wind of teaching arising from human trickery, from their cunning in the interests of deceitful scheming. Rather, living the truth in love, we should grow in every way into the one who is the head, Christ, from whom the whole body, joined and held together by every supporting ligament, with the proper functioning of each part, brings about the body's growth and builds itself up in love."

10. Cf. Pope Francis, *Joy of the Gospel*, par. 99.

that of her sisters. However, she could use strategies like that of a hunger strike to ensure that church officials recognized the wisdom and authority of her position on matters pertaining to the norms of her religious community. Her vow of obedience to God and her vow of obedience to Francis at times conflicted directly with what she was told to do by hierarchical officials, as in the case of being told by Pope Gregory IX to adopt the form of life he had drawn up for the women rather than the form of life she, with Francis's counsel and support, had been living. The major conflict was over the community's embrace of absolute poverty.

Gregory IX actually met with Clare personally about this. While he was in Assisi for the canonization of Francis, he visited Clare at San Damiano to get her to receive gifts of property he wanted to give her to secure the community's stability. Clare's refusal was firm and clear, as several of the sisters who witnessed the encounter affirmed in later testimony. According to Sister Benvenuta of Perugia: "Neither Pope Gregory nor the Bishop of Ostia could ever make her consent to receive any possessions." When asked for details, Sister Benvenuta said that she had been "present and heard the Lord Pope tell [Clare] that he wanted her to receive possessions."[11] Sister Pacifica confirms this, saying that Clare

> could never be persuaded to desire anything for herself, or to receive any possession for herself or the monastery. . . . Lord Pope Gregory . . . wanted to give her many things and buy possessions for the monastery. But she would never consent.[12]

If Gregory's actions sound paternalistic, they were informed by his keen grasp of local politics and jurisdiction. Having already ruled in several other cases around the region, he was aware of the dangers to the sisters' safety, the possibility that Franciscan brothers would not assist them in providing for their needs, and the reality that the

---

11. See "The Second Witness," in *Acts of the Process of Canonization*, 22, in Armstrong, *The Lady*, 155. The Bishop of Ostia was the Cardinal Protector of the Franciscans prior to becoming Pope Alexander IV.

12. See "The First Witness," in *Acts of the Process of Canonization*, 13, in Armstrong, *The Lady*, 147.

well-being of the Poor Ladies was not necessarily the highest priority on anyone's agenda—whether it was their local bishop or the faithful people of the area.[13] Further, the papal-imperial conflict had escalated, leading to further violence between Assisi and Perugia. The pope could not guarantee the safety of the holy women residing in the Spoleto valley. Speaking quietly with Clare, he even offered to absolve her of her vow of obedience to Francis if she was concerned about any possibility of violating something he had told her to do. Clare's reply was unequivocal: "Holy Father, I have absolutely no desire ever to be absolved from the following of Christ."[14]

The Franciscan tradition teaches us that the lens of poverty gives us a privileged view of the presence of God; this is one of the reasons that Clare, like Francis, clung to poverty so fiercely, defending it as the cornerstone on which an authentic gospel life is built. But poverty is not simply a means to see God; poverty provides us with a new honesty about our human limitations. Poverty is the recognition that, in and of ourselves, each of us is insufficient. This disposition of humility opens us to the constant surprise of God's presence and activity in our midst. Our orientation to the suffering poor in a world of violence and injustice, attunes us to "the saving power at work in their lives" and, as Pope Francis reminds us, "we need to let ourselves be evangelized by them." Our own simplicity and solidarity manifest our commitment to upholding the presence of God in, through, and with the poor of the

---

13. See discussion in Mueller, *Privilege of Poverty*, 32–39.

14. Clare's example is noteworthy: when confronted with an order—even one from the pope—that Clare believed compromised the integrity of her lived witness to God and to the spirit of Francis, she did not acquiesce to it. Uncompromisingly, she clung to the life of radical poverty and solidarity that exemplified the gospel's demands. The strength of her commitment and the great respect the pope had for her carried the day. Gregory IX granted Clare's request to be free from possessions in a letter traditionally known as the "Privilege of Poverty" on September 17, 1228, which states: "Therefore, we confirm with our apostolic authority, as you requested, your proposal of most high poverty, granting you by the authority of [those] present that no one can compel you to receive possessions." See Armstrong, *The Lady*, 87. Joan Mueller helps us decode the careful wording of this document: "Gregory did not permit Clare to 'have no possessions whatsoever,' as she had asked, but rather said that she could not 'be compelled by anyone to receive possessions.' Clare's desire for radical poverty was a rare spiritual gift, and Gregory wanted to ensure that the monastery would be able to acquire possessions as needed in the future. He worded his privilege in such a way that the sisters would easily be able to accept possessions without the embarrassment of having to ask the Apostolic See to take back the very privilege that they had so fervently requested." Mueller, *Privilege of Poverty*, 40.

world, who "have much to teach us. . . . We are called to find Christ in them, to lend our voice to their causes, but also to be their friends, to listen to them . . . and to embrace the mysterious wisdom which God wishes to share with us through them."[15]

Francis and Clare ask us, simply and plainly, to "embrace the poor Christ," because this is the most authentic expression of our relational commitment, to God and to others. Consequently, relationship with the poor Christ is the most trustworthy source of authority in our life as friends and disciples of Jesus.[16] And they ask us to be uncompromising, both in our commitment and in our tenderness,

---

15. Pope Francis, *Joy of the Gospel*, par. 198.
16. Cf. "In fact, if someone gives you contrary instructions or tempts you with anything that might hinder your perfection or seems contrary to your divine vocation, even if he is a person you must respect, still, do not follow his advice. Instead, poor virgin, embrace the Poor Christ." Clare of Assisi, "Second Letter to Agnes of Prague," in Mueller, *Privilege of Poverty*, 70. And earlier Clare writes:

> What you hold, may you [always] hold,
> What you do, may you do and not stop.
>> But with swift pace, light step, unswerving feet,
>> so that even your steps stir up no dust,
>> may you go forward securely, joyfully, and swiftly,
>> on the path of prudent happiness,
>> believing nothing,
>>> agreeing with nothing
>>> that would dissuade you from this commitment
>>> or would place a stumbling block for you on the way,
>> so that nothing prevents you from offering
>>> your vows to the Most High in the perfection
>>> to which the Spirit of the Lord has called you.

Clare of Assisi, "Second Letter to Agnes of Prague," 17–18 in Armstrong, *The Lady*, 48. See variant translation in Mueller, *Clare of Assisi*, 29, which has "trusting in no one and agreeing with no one because he might want to dissuade you from your founding purpose or might place a stumbling block in your way." While this is excellent general counsel, Clare wrote this letter to Agnes in direct response to another situation in which obedience to papal authority threatened to compromise the integrity of Agnes's solidarity with the poor. As Mueller glosses this text she notes: "The 'someone' Clare referred to was, of course, Pope Gregory himself. Clare knew only too well from her own experience with Gregory that he was not patient with those who declined to obey his commands under the pretense of following a higher authority. She knew that if Agnes persisted in her dedication to absolute poverty despite Gregory's command to the contrary, Agnes would suffer papal contempt. Because Agnes had become contemptible in this world, her source of strength must be the Lord, who became contemptible for the sake of humankind. . . . Agnes, although she would no doubt suffer the pain of contempt, was remaining true to her vocation to embrace the Poor Christ." Mueller, *Privilege of Poverty*, 70–71. In a letter dated May 18, 1235, Gregory IX had attached the hospice that had been built with Agnes's dowry, as well as its extensive assets and any possessions it should acquire, to her convent. This letter, in effect, forced Agnes to accept an endowment for her monastery—throwing her into the same dilemma that Clare had negotiated earlier: how was she to remain faithful to her vocation in God to be one with the poor Christ, especially given the irony that it was the vicar of Christ himself who seemed to be placing the stumbling block in the way? Because Clare knew just how delicate the

aware of the many ways that our partnership with God, particularly as it expresses itself through poverty and at the margins, can be undermined by the world and even by affiliations with those who claim to have our best interests at heart—be they family members, friends, or religious superiors. It takes both freedom and fortitude to seek God, as John of the Cross attests: "Seeking God demands a heart, naked, strong and free from all evils and goods that are not purely God."[17]

We, too, can seek God in the concrete ways that Francis and Clare did: through encounter and conversion, which then lead to solidarity and communion. Clare's four verbs, so helpful in establishing the prayerful relationship we establish with God and others, also show us how that prayer relationship takes action in the world around us. The God who speaks to us in the suffering of our sisters and brothers asks us to act upon what we learn as we gaze, consider, and contemplate the suffering Christ in our world today.

Relationship with that God will lead us to make choices. Each of those choices must be made toward the flourishing of our "divine vocation"—that is, faithful to the call of God to keep growing into our partnership with God and the demands of the gospel life as they speak to the challenges in our world today. The gospel invitation to new life is Christ's call to a new way of seeing reality and a whole new identity in which we are truly sister and brother to all. Each of us is called into covenantal relationship with God, and together we are called to live the way Jesus did—with deepest sensitivity to the stories and needs of the marginalized and deep commitment to eradicate exclusion and to live as one people. Pope Francis has actually coined a phrase to describe this: "*la mística de vivir juntos*" (the mystery of living together), a holy mystery that requires us to discover God in the messiness of our own midst.[18] And he says quite frankly:

situation was, she knew Agnes needed inner fortitude, strategic advice, and clarity with respect to principles of authority.

17. John of the Cross, "Spiritual Canticle," in *The Collected Works of St. John of the Cross*, trans. Kieran Kavanaugh and Otilio Rodriguez (Washington, DC: Institute of Carmelite Studies, 1979), 332. Interestingly, we should note that John's words suggest that not everything that can pull our focus from God is evil. In fact, it may even appear or even be something neutral or good in and of itself, but its effect on us is negative if and when it diverts or distracts us from the immediacy of our relationship with God.

Any Christian community, if it thinks it can comfortably go its own way without concern and effective cooperation in helping the poor to live with dignity and reaching out to everyone, will also risk breaking down, however much it may talk about social issues or criticize governments. It will easily drift into a spiritual worldliness camouflaged by religious practices, unproductive meetings and empty talk.[19]

What all of this reveals is simple: Our aspiration to image God in the world around us is not, and cannot be, solely an individual pursuit. Our communities, too, must emanate the reality of God's presence, and this is going to mean opening ourselves to the education and deep transformation that will happen as we stand at the margins of society, in solidarity and kinship, until the margins cease to exist. The "divine vocation" to which we are all called is a calling that grasps our individuality and our relatedness.

Humanity's vocation is thus to participate in God's communion for us . . . to live as Jesus Christ did. . . . Living such a life entails living in compassion and solidarity (being-with), living as a reconciling, forgiving presence; practicing hospitality to the stranger and outcast; and embracing all in love.[20]

Such an approach to community sacralizes us and our world as a process of growth, maturation, and grace. As Parker Palmer writes:

What we need is not simply the individual at prayer, seeking to stand in his or her own sacred space. We need a corporate practice that seeks a space in which we can all stand together. We need to know that God wants to bring us together as God's people and that we must listen to each other, in the words and in the silences between them, testing our own truth against the truth received by others. We need to know that God will work a greater truth in all of us standing together than can be worked in any one of us standing alone.[21]

18. Pope Francis, *Joy of the Gospel*, par. 87. This challenge contrasts with attitudes within Christian communities that Pope Francis criticizes, e.g.: "In some people we see an ostentatious preoccupation for the liturgy, for doctrine and for the Church's prestige, but without any concern that the Gospel have [sic] a real impact on God's faithful people and the concrete needs of the present time." Ibid., par. 95.

19. Pope Francis, *Joy of the Gospel*, par. 207.

20. Mark S. Medley, *Imago Trinitatis: Toward a Relational Understanding of Becoming Human* (Lanham, MD: University Press of America, 2002), 46. Cf. Catherine LaCugna, *God for Us: The Trinity and Christian Life* (HarperSanFrancisco, 1993), 382–88.

21. Palmer, *Promise of Paradox*, 91–92.

Christian communities should see this movement toward the fruition of humanity's potential as the restoration of the image of God that the Judeo-Christian tradition holds is an intrinsic part of our created nature. We noted the scriptural and theological grounding of this reality (Gen 1:26–27) last chapter. We are created in the image of God, which is to say that we bear that image in our being. We ought always to try to align our interpersonal relations with the image of God that we are called to embody and emanate into the world. Within the Christian tradition, we understand Christ to have restored that image from its fallen state. We could even say that Christ enlivened that image, so that, in Christ, with Christ, we can come to live in that image, individually and as a community. Douglas John Hall reminds us that "to be *imago Dei* does not mean to have something, but to be and do something: to image God."[22] Hall's use of the word "image" as a verb helps us to consider that the divine image and likeness is not just a thing, but also a living presence engaged in a relational process; it is neither an endowment nor a quality that humankind possesses. Rather it is an actual orientation of our very being that helps us to become something more than ourselves; it is in this orientation and this process that we are graced to image God in all our relationships.[23] It is through relationship that we become more fully human, we grow into God's life in us, and we realize more fully the image of God that we are.

Further, the mystery and beauty of God's creation—especially God's indwelling presence within all that God has created—become less accessible to us when we lack a direct and attentive relationship with all of creation. Our own experience bears that out at so many levels. It is hard to appreciate the mystery of a seed coming to life, growing into a plant, and subsequently providing food for us when we have never harvested a vegetable garden. It is hard to feel the grace of communion when we pick up a meal from a drive-through and wolf it down in our car on the way to the next errand. We become blinded to the

22. Douglas John Hall, *Imaging God: Dominion as Stewardship* (Grand Rapids: Eerdmans, 1986), 98.
23. Cf. Ibid., 2.

beauty that permeates our world when we are not in direct contact with its contours, landscapes, elements, and species, and when the web of creation itself is perilously unraveled by our habits of extraction and consumption. Each careless human practice fits into a larger jigsaw puzzle of deception until we fail to recognize how complicit we are in environmental deterioration and even human degradation.[24] The reality of God, which is the reality that Francis and Clare invite us to explore, is rooted in communities of graced generosity that know how to appreciate, sustain, and share their beauty and resources.

> The living God is the God who is alive in relationship, alive in communion with the creature, alive with desire for union with every creature. God is so thoroughly involved in every detail of creation that if we could truly grasp this it would altogether change how we approach each moment of our lives.[25]

Toward the end of his life, wracked by pain and blind from trachoma, Francis composed the Canticle of the Creatures, a hymn of praise and gratitude for the beauty and gifts of creation. Francis envisioned all of creation as united in bonds of affection and mutual interdependence. Sister Water, for example, he envisioned as "useful and humble and precious and pure." Pope Francis appeals to Saint Francis's vision as he contemplates a strained and wounded planet at the outset of his encyclical *Laudato Si': On Care for Our Common Home*:

> St. Francis is the example par excellence of care for the vulnerable and of an integral ecology lived out joyfully and authentically. He is the patron saint of all who study and work in the area of ecology, and he is also much loved by non-Christians. He was particularly concerned for God's creation and for the poor and outcast. He loved, and was deeply loved for his joy, his generous self-giving, his openheartedness. He was a mystic and a pilgrim who lived in simplicity and in wonderful harmony with God, with others, with nature and with himself. He shows us just how inseparable the bond is between concern for nature, justice for the poor, commitment to society, and interior peace. Francis helps us to see that an integral ecology . . . takes us to the heart of what it is to be human.[26]

24. See Pope Francis, *Laudato Si'*, par. 56.
25. LaCugna, *God for Us*, 304.
26. Pope Francis, *Laudato Si'*, par. 10–11.

In *On Care for Our Common Home*, Pope Francis points to two of the most profound instincts that Saint Francis offers us today. First, "Francis invites us to see nature as a magnificent book in which God speaks to us and grants us a glimpse of God's infinite beauty and goodness." He shows us that "rather than a problem to be solved, the world is a joyful mystery to be contemplated with gladness and praise."[27] Second, Saint Francis models a stern and profound resistance to cultural pressures to reduce people or nature into things to be consumed, as Pope Francis writes: "The poverty and austerity of St. Francis were no mere veneer of asceticism, but something much more radical: a refusal to turn reality into an object simply to be used and controlled."[28]

Both Pope Francis's *Joy of the Gospel* and his *Laudato Si': On Care for Our Common Home* envision practical ways that we can address the challenges we face today. In *On Care for Our Common Home*, Pope Francis explicitly asks us to move beyond "superficial rhetoric, sporadic acts of philanthropy and perfunctory expressions of concern for the environment"[29] in a paradigmatic shift with deep, transformative implications for us and for our world. Pope Francis calls for an "integral ecology," a sense of deep communion with all of creation that makes us

particularly indignant at the enormous inequalities in our midst, whereby we continue to tolerate some [people] considering themselves more worthy than others. We fail to see that some are mired in desperate and degrading poverty, with no way out, while others have not the faintest idea of what to do with their possessions, vainly showing off their supposed superiority and leaving behind them so much waste which, if it were the case everywhere, would destroy the planet. In practice, we continue to tolerate that some consider themselves more human than others, as if they had been born with greater rights.[30]

Clearly, this vision will require ongoing conversion in us, individually and communally, spurred on by our "loving awareness that we are not disconnected from the rest of creatures, but joined in a splendid universal communion."[31] Lamenting the fact that "people may well

27. Ibid., par. 12.
28. Ibid., par. 11.
29. Ibid., par. 54.
30. Ibid., par. 90.

have growing ecological sensitivity but it has not succeeded in changing their harmful habits of consumption which, rather than decreasing, appear to be growing all the more,"[32] Pope Francis asks all of us to recognize our relatedness to one another and to all creation, writing that our conversion must

> include the awareness that each creature reflects something of God and has a message to convey to us. . . . Then too, there is the recognition that God created the world, writing into it an order and a dynamism that human beings have no right to ignore. . . . I ask all Christians to recognize and live fully this dimension of their conversion. May the power and the light of the grace we have received also be evident in our relationship to other creatures and to the world around us. In this way, we will help nurture that sublime fraternity with all creation which St. Francis of Assisi so radiantly embodied.[33]

Francis and Clare model a clear conversion away from all that diminishes our human dignity, individually and collectively; they show us how to live with integrity and commitment to the values that matter, even when we are deprived of all else. Both their radical poverty and their tenderness, which gave them access to the full range of their humanity, set a standard for us as a people who choose to stand together in the constant and secretly interwoven relationships that bind us to one another. As we discover our intrinsic relatedness, we "not only marvel at the manifold connections existing among creatures, but also discover a key to our own fulfillment. The human person grows more, matures more and is sanctified more to the extent that he or she enters into relationships, going out from themselves to live in communion with God, with others and with all creatures."[34]

We require a new and universal solidarity. As the bishops of Southern

---

31. Ibid., par. 220. Pope Francis discusses the various elements of this conversion in ibid., par. 217–21, explicitly describing how Francis of Assisi models this conversion for us. See par. 218: "In calling to mind the figure of St. Francis of Assisi, we come to realize that a healthy relationship with creation is one dimension of overall personal conversion, which entails the recognition of our errors, sins, faults and failures, and leads to heartfelt repentance and desire to change." And again, par. 220: "This conversion calls for a number of attitudes which together foster a spirit of generous care, full of tenderness."
32. Ibid., par. 55.
33. Ibid., par. 221.
34. Ibid., par. 240.

Africa have stated: "Everyone's talents and involvement are needed to redress the damage caused by human abuse of God's creation." All of us can cooperate as instruments of God for the care of creation, each according to his or her own culture, experience, involvements and talents.[35]

There are many serious issues that need to be addressed and remediated. A new and universal solidarity would need to express itself in the cooperative construction of new systems of interaction, new ways of living together, along with legal frameworks that can guarantee human rights and a global ethos that demands and requires mutual accountabilities.[36] From human trafficking to gender-based violence and abuse to racism, exploitation, exclusion, and care for our fragile planet, we might find ourselves wondering where and how to begin. The injustices in our world easily spawn "a lethal absence of hope," and our task is to use God's own gaze at the spaces of horror and degradation to create new communities of vitality and life. Pope Francis puts this poignantly when he writes:

> How I wish that all of us would hear God's cry: "Where is your brother?" (Gn 4:9). Where is your brother or sister who is enslaved? Where is the brother and sister that you are killing each day in clandestine warehouses, in rings of prostitution, in children used for begging, in exploiting undocumented labor. Let us not look the other way. There is greater complicity than we think.[37]

The walls of exclusion in our own societies are strong enough to keep us from understanding or experiencing the richness on the other side of them. Encounter is what enriches our lives, and we will not discover that if we do not go beyond ourselves. If we recall Francis's initial experience in the leper colony, we remember that this was the space in which he himself was flooded with the love of God. What he expected

---

35. Ibid., par. 14.
36. Cf. Ibid., par. 53: "The problem is that we still lack the culture needed to confront this crisis. We lack leadership capable of striking out on new paths and meeting the needs of the present with concern for all and without prejudice toward coming generations. The establishment of a legal framework which can set clear boundaries and ensure the protection of ecosystems has become indispensable; otherwise, the new power structures based on the techno-economic paradigm may overwhelm not only our politics but also freedom and justice."
37. Pope Francis, *Joy of the Gospel*, par. 211.

to be a space of misery and abandonment was, to his surprise, a space of vitality, where human relatedness, care, and compassion had the capacity to change everything. It is the power of encounter that grounds Pope Francis's hope for us today when he writes:

> I hope that all communities will devote the necessary effort to advancing along the path of a pastoral and missionary conversion which cannot leave things as they presently are.[38]

Going forth, going out, to learn at the margins is the critical practice. The impulse of love is one of movement; Jesus went forth, involving himself in the guts of people's lives and asking others to get involved, too. As Pope Francis writes, "going forth" means taking the first step, being involved and supportive, bearing fruit and rejoicing. It means becoming a community that "gets involved by word and deed in people's daily lives; it bridges distances . . . and embraces human life, touching the suffering flesh of Christ in others."[39]

Clearly, a form of life rooted in poverty and lived at the margins is difficult and demanding. What does it have to offer us? Greg Boyle reminds us that the space of encounter is a space of privilege. Our voluntary displacement with the oppressed, with those whose burdens make it nearly impossible for them to even cry out for the help they need, gives us a life-changing perspective that we cannot find on our own:

> The poor give you a privileged access to the God who stands there with them. Once you experience this, it is where you want to reside. . . . If you listen to the poor and those on the margins, they will tell you what needs to be done.[40]

Out of the logic of the relationships that form at the margins, we can begin to sit down together and ask what our hopes and dreams look like as we explore them together. A profound vitality and creativity exists in that kind of honest journeying—one that the disciples on the

---

38. Ibid., par. 25.
39. Ibid., par 24.
40. Boyle, *Tattoos on the Heart*, 229, 225.

road to Emmaus knew as they looked at one another and asked, "Were not our hearts burning within us?" Indeed, if we were to sit down at a table, in a space where "there is no 'us' and 'them,' just 'us,'" holding up together the challenges and invitations that emerged, we would already be participating in the story of Francis and Clare and, more importantly, Jesus and his contemporaries. This is table ministry. This is the gospel life.

And tables are a great place to start. Whether we take our cues from Francis, Clare, or Jesus himself, we see that their most profound moments were probably shared in conversations around tables breaking bread. If we aspire to journey together and be companions to one another, it does not get much more basic than that. The problem is that our tables—and the food found there—are completely inaccessible to so many of the world's poor. In Luke, Jesus has sharp words for such exclusion. "When you hold a lunch or a dinner, do not invite your friends or your brothers and sisters or your families and wealthy neighbors, in case they may invite you back and you have repayment. Rather, when you hold a banquet invite the poor, the crippled, the lame, the blind; blessed indeed will you be" (Luke 14:12–14a). We might start by gazing around our own tables, noticing who is there, and realizing who is not. We might then gain a more sensitive awareness of what we are eating and with whom; how our food is being produced; who labors to harvest, process, and prepare it; what it costs to produce, distribute and consume it; and whether or not all of our sisters and brothers have access to it. And if not, why not.

I know very few human beings who would actually begrudge someone sitting next to them at the table a portion from the serving plate. But we are a long way, locally and globally, from this kind of solidarity, so very basic to Jesus's community and its table ministry. Solidarity around food—its production, preparation, consumption, and distribution—is a transforming practice that would promote justice, health, well-being, and greater habits of community. We live in a world that is even more sharply divided between the extremes of starvation and indulgence, and although many of us already know that the ways that we cultivate food contribute strongly and adversely to the environmental crisis, we have made surprisingly little progress in establishing food justice.

As Francis and Clare knew, what we choose to eat is not only a statement about our commitment to our personal well-being but is also an ethical stance with important implications for our social, economic, and political structures. When we add the economic and environmental costs of food production for our imbalanced diets, the moral importance of feeding ourselves wisely and with restraint as a practice of solidarity with the human community and with all of creation emerges in strong relief.[41] But neither ought our approach to food be completely dour. The sharing of meals, both in preparing them and in sharing them together, is a critical element of culture. The rise of a fast-food culture has had a detrimental impact on individual health and on communal and interpersonal well-being. In point of fact, the consumption of fast food is rarely satisfying, nutritionally or socially, and the conversations that originate in meal sharing are a critical part of the ecology of daily life.

Food justice illuminates a larger web of inequities in need of our attention. When we consider the direct connection between human trafficking and other abusive labor practices in certain food industries,[42] the many direct correlations between our approach to food and human suffering and exploitation would become obvious. As many Christian ethicists have pointed out, widespread ignorance among Christians about the causal connections between what we eat,

---

41. We cannot hope to achieve "sustainability" and control the greenhouse effect without drastic change in food production and consumption. More than a third of all raw materials and fossil fuels consumed in the United States are used in animal production, and it takes approximately 1,850 gallons of water (or 15,000 pounds) to grow a single pound of beef. See M. M. Mekonnen and A. Y. Hoekstra, "The Green, Blue and Gray Water Footprint of Farm Animals and Animal Products," Value of Water Research Report Series No. 48, UNESCO-IHE, Delft, 2010, p. 19. In her analysis of this issue Maude Barlow states that global meat production is predicted to double by 2050, using 70 percent of all agricultural lands and consuming one third of the world's grain. See Maude Barlow, *Blue Future: Protecting Water for People and the Planet Forever* (New York: New Press, 2014), 15. For a basic introduction to the energy and fossil fuel costs of the US food system, see David Wann, "Trimming the Fat: Farewell to Fossil Food," in *Simple Prosperity: Finding Real Wealth in a Sustainable Lifestyle* (New York: St. Martin's Press, 2007), 198–211.
42. For an introduction, see, for example, Robert Gottlieb and Anupama Joshi, *Food Justice* (Cambridge: MIT Press, 2010), 13–35.

where it comes from, and how it is produced, on the one hand, and social justice on the other, is no longer easily excusable. Food is only one industry that needs our scrutiny and consideration. I use it here as emblematic of how our ethical ideals are often, in reality, thoroughly undermined by our own complicity in an unjust world—a complicity we often do not recognize until gazing, considering, and contemplating leads us to conversion and a thorough imitation and sharing of the love that gives life. It is basic but it also becomes revolutionary.

This same process of gazing around our tables and becoming more cognizant of who we exclude from the conversation applies to our corporate, governmental, economic, and ecclesial tables.

> It needs to be said that, generally speaking, there is little in the way of clear awareness of problems which especially affect the excluded. Yet they are the majority of the planet's population, billions of people. These days, they are mentioned in international political and economic discussions, but one often has the impression that their problems are brought up as an afterthought, a question which gets added almost out of duty or in a tangential way, if not treated merely as collateral damage. . . . This is due partly to the fact that many professionals, opinion makers, communications media and centers of power, being located in affluent urban areas, are far removed from the poor, with little direct contact with their problems. . . . Their lack of physical contact and encounter, encouraged at times by the disintegration of our cities, can lead to a numbing of conscience and to tendentious analyses which neglect parts of reality.[43]

As Pope Francis reminds us, including everyone not only at the table but in our analysis and understanding of our own reality, is critical to the well-being of all of us. Our decisions and actions, especially those with far-reaching geographical and historical consequences, must be made on the basis of accurate information, gathered from those whose lived experience give them unique insight into our problems and their possible solutions.

We live in the context of challenges that require us to change. We can throw up our hands at the Babel of our world or we can challenge ourselves to reclaim together all that is lost through our insensitivities,

43. Pope Francis, *Laudato Si': On Care for Our Common Home*, par. 49.

indifference, and intransigence. Deeply integral to the "revolution of tenderness" that Pope Francis calls for and the practice of tenderness that Francis and Clare modeled is the quality of our human interactions. The *communio* that we have described is one that can and ought to exist in every sphere of human interaction, beginning with our closest and most intimate relationships, where we learn the tenderness that is "a sign of a love free of selfish possessiveness. It makes us approach a person with immense respect and a certain dread of causing them harm or taking away their freedom. Loving another person involves the joy of contemplating and appreciating their innate beauty and sacredness, which is greater than my needs."[44]

God's tenderness is meant to manifest itself in all of our forms of human relatedness as an integral part of our journey as human beings. Its hallmarks are justice, dignity, mutual respect, and powerful cherishing. And the times in which we live demand this tenderness with a new and powerful urgency.

Francis and Clare invite us into a way of life in which loving others is a desire that unites us to God and stems naturally from the knowledge that we are loved. It is a way of loving grown in us as we come to understand that we are all sisters and brothers, children of the same Source. Greg Boyle describes our core relatedness very simply, calling it "kinship," which he defines as what happens to us when we refuse to forget that we belong to each other. "With kinship as the goal," he writes, "other essential things fall into place; without it, no justice, no peace. I suspect that were kinship our goal, we would no longer be promoting justice—we would be celebrating it."[45] Kinship is not service and it is not charity. Kinship, like solidarity, is mutuality, known as we share vulnerability, joy, challenges, hopes, dreams, and desires. It is the shared space where the tenderness that formed us calls us home.

44. Pope Francis, *The Joy of Love* (Washington, DC: United States Conference of Catholic Bishops, 2016), par. 127.
45. Boyle, *Tattoos on the Heart*, 187.

Epilogue: Let the Revolution Begin!

Christ's resurrection is not an event of the past; it contains a vital power which has permeated this world. Where all seems to be dead, signs of the resurrection suddenly spring up. It is an irresistible force. Often it seems that God does not exist: all around us we see persistent injustice, evil, indifference and cruelty. But it is also true that in the midst of darkness something new always springs to life and sooner or later produces fruit. On razed land life breaks through, stubbornly yet invincibly. . . . Each day in our world beauty is born anew, it rises transformed through the storms of history. Values always tend to reappear under new guises, and human beings have arisen time after time from situations that seemed doomed. Such is the power of the resurrection, and all who evangelize are instruments of that power. (Pope Francis, *Joy of the Gospel*, par. 276)

The legacy of Francis and Clare is their invitation into an authentic, all-encompassing, gospel-informed way of life. This legacy is grounded in a God-centered vision of humanity and the world that manifests and engenders tenderness, reverence, justice, simplicity, peace, and joy.

A fundamental element of Francis and Clare's way of life is its relational orientation. Nothing created is complete in and of itself; each and every creature is seen as reflective of its creator. Each and every person is a manifestation and a mirror of the divine presence that loved it into being. And, as one is gradually drawn into the reality of that divine presence, one enters into the fullness of the Trinitarian life, one that engenders liberty and loving relationship in the other.[1]

---

1. See Leonardo Boff, *Francis of Assisi: A Model for Human Liberation* (Maryknoll, NY: Orbis, 2006), 67. I have added "loving relationship" to his description of Francis's sense of relationship as one that "engenders liberty in the other."

Francis and Clare's relational way of life shows us how to be together in human community. Leonardo Boff might help us initially understand that way of being together with his challenge: "Francis has left us with a serious question: is it possible, as he tried to do, for any group to live the Gospel utopia of radical poverty as a way of achieving a real fraternity?"[2] But Francis and Clare lived and experienced not only radical poverty but also radical joy and even abundance of divine presence. While we cannot and ought not minimize their suffering and privation, joyfully embraced and staunchly defended, we would misunderstand their experience of their own humanity if we saw it only in terms of poverty—material, spiritual, or human.

The paradox and mystery of Francis and Clare's poverty, like that of Christ, is that it completely redefines their experience of humanity. To live in poverty is to live in acute awareness of our need for God, our desire for God—and for one another. Francis and Clare's poverty is the poverty of incompletion that invites us into relational fullness, that draws us into a new identity, one defined by solidarity, mutuality and the dynamic awareness of being an integral part of something much greater than ourselves. The spirit of non-possessiveness releases in us the capacity to feel the presence of God, to completely "dispose" ourselves to that presence, resting in it and dwelling in it as our deepest, truest reality. Boff suggests that this form of human community "presupposes an ethical, humanitarian, and mystical desire"[3] that is unique to intentional communities who courageously commit themselves to intense and radical individual and communal transformation through the living power of the Holy Spirit. Such a thing is, Boff claims, "impossible to demand of a larger group," but, in smaller communities of intentionality, Francis and Clare show how this commitment becomes a living and vital reality: "Francis lived the *esprit de finesse*, the spirit of gentleness."[4]

Francis and Clare also have a great deal to teach us about the power of intentional relationship. Without the need for a great deal of

2. Ibid., 68.
3. Ibid., 71.
4. Ibid., ix; "the spirit of gentleness" comes from Blaise Pascal.

conversation or even contact, they were able to cultivate and nurture a profound and prayerful supportive relationship. In the quiet spaces of their own hearts, they knew that they could always find the loving prayers of the other to uphold them in their integrity and heart-felt sincerity to live out their relationship with God. Indeed, the union with God that each of them enjoyed was, in very real senses a shared union, a communion with one another. They come closest to touching the heart of sacramental relationship of any two people I know. If that tender, "providential" care and regard for the other were at the heart of every committed human relationship, our world would be a very different place. For the love that burned in each of their hearts was magnified by the knowledge that there was another human being on this earth who knew, understood, and revered that fire as sacred.

Knowing and experiencing this kind of love immediately pulls love out of the realm of sentimentality and restores it rightfully to its place of ultimate power. It is the kind of love that dispels the idolatrous ways that we perceive and enact power in our world.

As Pope Francis invites us to know and experience the power of tenderness, he tells us that "loving others is a spiritual force drawing us to union with God; indeed, one who does not love others 'walks in the darkness' (1 John 2:11), 'remains in death' (1 John 3:14) and 'does not know God (1 John 4:8)."[5] Love is, in the end, the only light that "can always illuminate a world grown dim and give us the courage needed to keep living and working. . . . We do not live better when we flee, hide, refuse to share, stop giving and lock ourselves up in our own comforts. Such a life is nothing less than a slow suicide."[6] Francis and Clare show us that meaning, purpose, and joy can only be found when hopes, dreams, challenges, and all the things that make us human are shared. The vitality they discovered in sharing God's dream to be known in all people is one that we, too, can discover today.

5. Pope Francis, *Joy of the Gospel*, par. 272.
6. Ibid.

Bibliography

Primary Sources

Armstrong, Regis J., ed. *The Lady: Clare of Assisi, Early Documents*. New York: New City Press, 2006.

Armstrong, Regis J., J. A. Wayne Hellmann, and William J. Short, eds., *The Founder*, vol. 2 of *Francis of Assisi: Early Documents*. New York: New City Press, 2000.

Armstrong, Regis J., J. A. Wayne Hellmann, and William J. Short, eds., *The Prophet*, vol. 3 of *Francis of Assisi: Early Documents*. New York: New City Press, 2001.

Armstrong, Regis J., J. A. Wayne Hellmann, and William J. Short, eds., *The Saint*, vol. 1 of *Francis of Assisi: Early Documents*. New York: New City Press, 1999.

Bonaventure. *The Soul's Journey into God, The Tree of Life, The Life of St. Francis*. Translated by Ewert Cousins. New York: Paulist Press, 1978.

Clare of Assisi. *Clare of Assisi: The Letters to Agnes*. Translated by Joan Mueller. Collegeville, MN: Michael Glazier, 2003.

Francis (Pope). *The Joy of Love*. Washington, DC: United States Conference of Catholic Bishops, 2016.

_____. *The Joy of the Gospel. Evangelii Gaudium*. Washington, DC: United States Conference of Catholic Bishops, 2013.

_____. *Laudato Si': On Care for Our Common Home*. Washington, DC: United States Conference of Catholic Bishops, 2015.

John of the Cross. *The Collected Works of St. John of the Cross*. Translated by Kieran

Kavanaugh and Otilio Rodriguez. Washington, DC: Institute of Carmelite Studies, 1979.

Loyola, Ignatius. *Draw Me into Your Friendship: The Spiritual Exercises, A Literal Translation and a Contemporary Reading.* Edited by David L. Fleming. St. Louis: The Institute of Jesuit Sources, 1996.

Teresa of Avila. *The Interior Castle.* Translated by Kieran Kavanaugh and Otilio Rodriguez. Mahwah, NJ: Paulist Press, 1979.

Secondary Sources on Francis and Clare

Alberzoni, Maria Pia. *Clare of Assisi and the Poor Sisters in the Thirteenth Century.* St. Bonaventure, NY: Franciscan Institute Publications, 2004.

Bodo, Murray. *The Way of St. Francis: The Challenge of Franciscan Spirituality for Everyone.* New York: Image Books, 1985.

Boff, Leonardo. *Francis of Assisi: A Model for Human Liberation.* Translated by John W. Diercksmeier. Maryknoll, NY: Orbis Books, 2006.

Carney, Margaret. *The First Franciscan Woman: Clare of Assisi and Her Form of Life.* Quincy, IL: Franciscan Press, 1993.

Dalarun, Jacques. *Francis of Assisi and Power.* St. Bonaventure, NY: Franciscan Institute Publications, 2007.

_____. *Francis of Assisi and the Feminine.* St. Bonaventure, NY: Franciscan Institute Publications, 2006.

_____. *The Misadventure of Francis of Assisi: Toward a Historical Use of the Franciscan Legends.* St. Bonaventure, NY: Franciscan Institute Publications, 2002.

Dalarun, Jacques, Michael F. Cusato, and Carla Salvati. *The Stigmata of Francis of Assisi: New Studies, New Perspectives.* St. Bonaventure, NY: Franciscan Institute Publications, 2006.

Delio, Ilia. *Clare of Assisi: A Heart Full of Love.* Cincinnati: St. Anthony Messenger Press, 2007.

_____. *Franciscan Prayer.* Cincinnati: St. Anthony Messenger Press, 2004.

_____. *A Franciscan View of Creation: Learning to Live in a Sacramental World.* St. Bonaventure, NY: Franciscan Institute Publications, 2003.

Delio, Ilia, Keith Douglass Warner, and Pamela Wood. *Care for Creation: A*

Franciscan Spirituality of the Earth. Cincinnati: St. Anthony Messenger Press, 2008.

Desbonnets, Théophile. *From Intuition to Institution: The Franciscans*. Chicago: Franciscan Herald Press, 1988.

Flood, D., and T. Matura. *The Birth of a Movement: A Study of the First Rule of St. Francis*. Chicago: Franciscan Herald Press, 1975.

Fortini, Arnaldo. *Francis of Assisi*. Translated by Helen Moak. New York: Crossroad, 1981.

_____. *Nova Vita di San Francesco*. Milan: Alpes, 1926.

Frugoni, Chiara. *Francis of Assisi: A Life*. New York: Continuum, 1998.

House, Adrian. *Francis of Assisi: A Revolutionary Life*. Mahwah, NJ: Paulist Press, 2001.

Lambert, Malcolm D. *Franciscan Poverty: The Doctrine of the Absolute Poverty of Christ and the Apostles in the Franciscan Order (1210–1323)*. St. Bonaventure, NY: Franciscan Institute Publications, 1998.

Manselli, Raoul. *Saint Francis of Assisi*. Chicago: Franciscan Herald Press, 1988.

Mueller, Joan. *The Privilege of Poverty: Clare of Assisi, Agnes of Prague, and the Struggle for a Franciscan Rule for Women*. University Park: Pennsylvania State University Press, 2006.

Spoto, Donald. *Reluctant Saint*. New York: Viking Compass, 2002.

Other Resources

Ahlgren, Gillian T. W. *Enkindling Love: The Legacy of Teresa of Avila and John of the Cross*. Minneapolis: Fortress Press, 2016.

_____. *Entering Teresa of Avila's* Interior Castle: *A Reader's Companion*. Mahwah, NJ: Paulist Press, 2005.

Athanasius. *The Life of Antony and the Letter to Marcellinus*. Translated by Robert C. Gregg. New York: Paulist Press, 1980.

Barlow, Maude. *Blue Future: Protecting Water for People and the Planet Forever*. New York: New Press, 2014.

Boyle, Gregory. *Tattoos on the Heart: The Power of Boundless Compassion*. New York: Free Press, 2010.

Brock, Rita Nakashima. *Journeys by Heart: A Christology of Erotic Power*. New York: Crossroad, 1988.

Castner, Brian. *The Long Walk: A Story of War and the Life That Follows.* New York: Anchor, 2012.

Downey, Michael. "Compassion." In *Dictionary of Catholic Spirituality,* 192. Collegeville, MN: Michael Glazier, 1993.

Dunson, Donald. *No Room at the Table: Earth's Most Vulnerable Children.* Maryknoll, New York: Orbis Press, 2003.

Gottlieb, Robert and Anupama Joshi. *Food Justice.* Cambridge: MIT Press, 2010.

Hall, Douglas John. *Imaging God: Dominion as Stewardship.* Grand Rapids: Eerdmans, 1986.

Hedges, Chris. *War is a Force that Gives Us Meaning.* New York: Public Affairs, 2002.

Jones, Alan. *Soul Making: The Desert Way of Spirituality.* San Francisco: HarperSanFrancisco, 1989.

Kasper, Walter. *Mercy: The Essence of the Gospel and the Key to Christian Life.* Translated by William Madges. Mahwah, NJ: Paulist Press, 2014.

Little, Lester K. *Religious Poverty and the Profit Economy in Medieval Europe.* Ithaca, NY: Cornell University Press, 1978.

McGinn, Bernard. *The Flowering of Mysticism: Men and Women in the New Mysticism—1200-1350.* New York: Crossroad, 1998.

_____. *The Foundations of Mysticism: Origins to the Fifth Century.* New York: Crossroad, 1991.

Medley, Mark S. *Imago Trinitatis: Toward a Relational Understanding of Becoming Human.* Lanham, MD: University Press of America, 2002.

Nelson Wieman, Henry. *The Source of Human Good.* Carbondale: Southern Illinois University Press, 1967.

Nolan, Albert. *Jesus before Christianity.* Maryknoll, NY: Orbis: 2003.

Nouwen, Henri J. M. *Life of the Beloved: Spiritual Living in a Secular World.* New York: Crossroad, 1992.

O'Donohue, John. *Beauty: The Invisible Embrace.* New York: HarperCollins, 2004.

_____. *Eternal Echoes: Exploring Our Hunger to Belong.* New York: Bantam, 2000.

Palmer, Parker. *Let Your Life Speak: Listening for the Voice of Vocation.* San Francisco: Jossey-Bass, 2000.

_____. *The Promise of Paradox: A Celebration of Contradictions in the Christian Life.* San Francisco: Jossey-Bass, 2008.

Sayers, Jane E. *Innocent III: Leader of Europe 1198–1216.* New York: Longman, 1994.

Teilhard de Chardin, Pierre. *The Making of a Mind: Letters from a Soldier Priest, 1914–1919.* Translated by René Hague. New York: Harper and Row, 1965.

Trible, Phyllis. *God and the Rhetoric of Sexuality.* Philadelphia: Fortress Press, 1978.

Wann, David. *Simple Prosperity: Finding Real Wealth in a Sustainable Lifestyle.* New York: St. Martin's Press, 2007.

Index of Names and Places

Index of Subjects